THE ART OF THE THEATRE

The Art of the Theatre

By HENRI GHÉON

Translated by ADELE M. FISKE
Introduction by MICHEL SAINT-DENIS

A DRAMABOOK

 HILL AND WANG – NEW YORK

Copyright © 1961 by the Estate of Henri Ghéon
Library of Congress Catalog Card Number: 61-6944

The translator of *The Art of the Theatre,* Adele M. Fiske,
R.S.C.J., is professor of Classics at Manhattanville College and
faculty advisor to the Dramatic Association there. The transla-
tion was made at the suggestion of the National Catholic Theatre
Conference. Adele M. Fiske has also translated plays of Paul
Claudel, Henri Ghéon, Diego Fabbri, and Georges Schéhade.

Manufactured in the United States of America by
The Colonial Press, Inc., Clinton, Massachusetts

PREFACE

In 1923, Jacques Copeau,[1] uncle of Michel Saint-Denis, asked Henri Ghéon to give some talks to a group of his actors, students, and friends. In these four talks, given in Copeau's theatre, the Vieux-Colombier, Ghéon discussed his concept of dramatic art, a concept very close to that of Copeau, and gave expression to the spirit of faith and of poetry in which he himself labored with love all his life, for beauty and high drama. The four talks compose this book, with the addition of an appendix added by Ghéon fifteen years later.

CONTENTS

INTRODUCTION

I KNEW Henri Ghéon for more than thirty years.
He belonged to the generation that preceded my own.
I knew him first as a member of the circle of writers and
artists of the Nouvelle Revue Française, the first circle to
which he belonged, and later as one of the Vieux-Colombier group. After the 1914-18 war, during which he was
converted to Catholicism, I followed Ghéon more and
more closely until, about 1933, we worked side by side
when I was performing his *Paysanne de Vallecas,* which
he had adapted from Tirso de Molina. After that it was
from an increasing distance that I followed his activities
as a man of the Catholic theatre; in the course of my trips
and my visits abroad I heard reports of the many performances he gave of his works, in England, Canada,
Belgium, Switzerland. Then in 1943-44, during the Occupation, Ghéon found means of getting a message
through to me from Morocco to London. A short time
after that he died, without my having seen him again.

During my fourth trip to the United States, in 1960,
I went to give a lecture at the College of the Sacred Heart
in the suburbs of New York, at the invitation of Mother

Fiske, who let me read the lectures which are published in this book: they had been delivered at the Vieux-Colombier while I was working there in 1923 and were put into finished form in 1938. That is how America suddenly put me in touch with my friend again.

I want to say a word first about Ghéon as a friend before I allude to his work.

Henri Ghéon was a man enriched with many gifts. His early life was complex until the time when, in his last twenty-five years, he seemed to have simplified it through the love of God and the encompassing practice of a dramatic art put at the service of religion.

To begin with, Ghéon is an assumed name. His real name was Doctor Henri Vangeon. He was a medical doctor, one who cared for the sick. I picture him as a country doctor, and I believe he was just that, in the suburbs of Paris. In any case he was an Army doctor through the First World War and found himself daily at grips with death and the sufferings of the wounded of whom he was in charge.

I believe I met Ghéon for the first time in 1907: it was on the isle of Jersey, where a group of friends from the Nouvelle Revue Française had decided to pass their summer holidays. Among others there were Jacques Copeau and André Gide. I remember Ghéon planted before an easel on the lawn; he was painting portraits and landscapes in oils. He never made a career of painting, but he knew how to handle pencils and brushes.

In 1913, or at the beginning of 1914, I attended a performance at the Vieux-Colombier of *L'Eau-de-Vie,* a tragedy of peasant life that Ghéon wrote in the secular period of his work; it was a sequel to another social drama, *Le Pain,* which had been produced about 1911 at Jacques Rouché's Théâtre des Arts. And then one evening about 1922 I went to the Théâtre Fontaine in Montmartre to see a performance of *La Farce du Pendu Dépendu,* also by Ghéon. He was there in the theatre himself, standing at the back of the balcony. I watched him as closely as I watched the performers. He was a show in himself. He had staged the play, and he was muttering his dialogue in a low voice, exactly in time with the actors' speech. He wasn't listening, he was acting, moving about incessantly. His face, which was very expressive, mimicked the expressions of all the characters; and he laughed sometimes, louder than all the rest, with that convulsive laugh of his, part strangulation, part cough, and part sneeze.

One day in 1932 he took me to his house to make me listen to some recordings he had selected from among the most inspired works of Mozart, for whom he had the greatest admiration. That was shortly before the publication of his great book on Mozart, which remains an authoritative work to this day.

In these anecdotes Dr. Vangeon, alias Henri Ghéon, appears under the combined aspects of dramatic author, director, painter, and music critic. From this we can begin to make out the man himself.

Ghéon was of middle height, full-bodied but muscular, with the physique of an active man; for he was very active physically, perpetually in motion, giving himself as passionately to the ideas he stood for as to the people he loved. He had a round face, regular features, eyes at once bright and gentle; but his florid compexion, often red, his brow smooth from premature baldness, and the mobility of his features gave him what is called in French *"une trogne"* (a mug). He made one think of a monk, or of a soldier, and of a certain type of actor or character, too—one might have placed him somewhere between Pierrot and Puechinello. He was made up of gentleness and of ferocity. As he says himself, he took to heart every one of his convictions; with great courage he put himself completely at their service. He was incapable of disloyalty or of indifference, whatever situation he was in. In no way narrowly sectarian, he was deliberately partisan.

Young people could approach Ghéon easily. He didn't intimidate them; there was nothing aloof about this intellectual. You were at once on an equal footing with him, or so you felt. That impression resulted from the ardent *joy* that Ghéon emanated, a delight, which he derived not so much from living as from exchanging ideas, communicating; he communicated with human beings, with works of art, with things, by a process at once animal and spiritual, so that sometimes he reached a level of exaltation that was almost frightening. Perhaps his lucidity toward himself suffered sometimes from these states. And yet Ghéon was also gifted with a great common sense, a common sense of the people, which was allied to a humility bordering on candor. Copeau made fun of him when Ghéon told how, during the war, noticing an ordinary statue of the Virgin suspended in the ruins of a bombed church, he had fallen to his knees to believe and to worship. He liked to humiliate his reason like that. Copeau made fun of him, and admired him.

The man whom I have just described was brought back

to my mind when I read the text published here, in which one rediscovers his complete personality, with his intransigence, his exaltation that blazed up in heated moments, but also with his calm critical clear-headedness. Ghéon couldn't help that discrepancy, but he knew how to reconcile these extremes in himself. All the men of the Nouvelle Revue Française turned, between 1900 and 1910, to a critical scrutiny, a rigorous re-examination of the values of their time. All of them, in every field of art, were eminent critics, and among them Ghéon, after his book *Nos Directions,* was considered one of the foremost.

In his lectures at the Vieux-Colombier he speaks as a critic, in spite of what he says; but this critic is, of course, also a man of action. He already knew the theatre: does he not claim the right to speak to us "as a writer, a producer, and even a businessman?" In fact he is going to define his dramatic doctrine; but he is no pedant, he will make his doctrine grow little by little out of the vast inclusive panorama of the theatre's evolution which he manages to spread before us. Ghéon will focus particularly on the French theatre from the Middle Ages to 1938, but he will go as far back as the Greeks, and he will cover what is essential in the European theatre. If the reader takes issue with Ghéon's views and judgments and with some of his conclusions in the course of this voyage across the history of dramatic art, it will generally be because he is unable to agree with the author's very premise. And I think it is necessary to be on guard against assuming that Ghéon's adherence to the Catholic church inspired his ideas fundamentally. His ideas on dramatic art antedated his conversion; they had already influenced him when he was writing the early plays, *Le Pain* and *L'Eau-de-Vie.*

Rooted at the heart of the convictions of Ghéon the secular dramatist was the idea of a popular theatre. In essence dramatic art is popular, which is to say open, accessible to everybody, striving toward a communion between the public and the stage. But the word "popular" does not imply "vulgar"; the man who ought to rule the stage is the author. Although Ghéon deplored the divorce between literature and the drama, he ruled off the stage both the novelist, whose diffuse developments are too much akin to everyday life, and the formal, or subjective, poet as well. The writer whom Ghéon summons to take the lead in dramatic art, and who is closely accompanied by his double the actor, is, however, a poet; but a poet of the theatre, and the actor is his incarnation. So Ghéon goes on to pursue a definition of what he calls a poetry of the theatre, and to define for us by many examples the difficult notion of style. He writes (page 50 f.), "Until the day of the bourgeois theatre all playwrights had been poets not because they wrote in verse—look at Molière—but because they transposed reality to a new level of order, harmony, simplicity, by rhythmic beauty, plastic beauty, and freedom. . . . The stage is a mirror in which reality sees itself not in its fleeting appearance, but in its abiding, eternal depths . . . [*a different concept of space,* not enclosed within four walls, *a different concept of time,* not measured by our watches, *a language of sign.* . .] . Such was and such is the theatre; such it has been in all times, under all skies, and such should be today what I call the poetry of the theatre."

"Style, the poetry proper to the theatre," Ghéon writes (page 63), insisting in this that from such poetry true style is born, that the one merges with the other. What is important is the nature of the imagination expressed by the text. Ghéon is himself above all a writer: to him the text "is the kernel, the mother cell, and nothing can replace it. . . ." And he adds, "But granted that, we must also hold that drama has its own thought which is not that of poetry or of the novel, thought that must escape the written word if it is to have any life or power. . . . When the playwright has trapped in written words the always relative absolute of his vision, that dream-group of personalities who meet, love, hate, live, and die at his good pleasure—he has as yet done nothing. He owes it to his art and to himself to design a dream that is realizable, viable, playable, and, if I may coin a pretty poor word, 'exteriorizable.' I repeat, he must not say, 'Here are words, give them life, form, gesture, movement, action!' If that were enough, a scenario would do and drama would amount to no more than that embryo called *commedia dell'arte*. His very words must of themselves evoke image, gesture, movement, action, life; to add all this afterward is a poor artifice."

You see how definite and demanding Ghéon is. It is clear that he is putting a popular art on a very high level; there is no question here of his adapting himself to the level of the populace. Personally I think the improvised form of the *commedia dell'arte* attained a meaning and a scenic power of as great value as any written text, but unfortunately it is ephemeral, not transmittable to posterity, and so its standing is inferior.

Ghéon writes, on page 12, "All art is essentially social,"

for he is concerned with the means of communication between his art and the public, whose presence and attention are as essential as the actor's. Ghéon thirsted for
the absolute in an age of relative values: he took to heart
the statements that Jacques Copeau made later, that
"There will never be a new theatre until the day comes
when the man in the audience murmurs in his heart and
with his heart the same words spoken by the man on the
stage." To the question Ghéon asked (page 78)—"Perhaps the basis of understanding is man himself?"—he
answered: No, not with modern man. That is why he
found his satisfaction and, I hope, his fullest flowering
in writing for an essentially Catholic public; there he
could hope for unanimity, and what is more important
for a Catholic than communion in the faith? If in doing
so, Ghéon was yielding to the dictates of his heart, nonetheless it was in the logic of his intellectual progress. He
hoped to probe more deeply into the field of his work
by limiting its scope. Did he not sense the danger of
this? Didn't he feel some regret when he wrote (page
82), "The presentation of evil may be somewhat restricted . . ."? But he consoles himself by adding,
". . . art flourishes under restraint."

Whether this doctrine pre-existed and provided him
with his views on theatre history, or whether the history
engendered the doctrine, it is clear from the first that the
only period Ghéon wholly rejected as contrary to the
very laws of theatre is the naturalistic period. Of the
French classics he really accepted none but Molière, and
even of Molière he preferred the works in prose. To the
others, from Corneille to Marivaux, he grants the attri-

butes of style and sound dramatic method, but he re-
proaches them for having begot, little by little, the
"closed" theatre from which the people are excluded.

For Ghéon the great highway of world theatre starts
with the Greeks, with Aeschylus and Sophocles more
than Euripides; then it vanishes for a time, to reappear
in the Middle Ages, which produced no masterpiece in
France but which did produce the Golden Age in Spain,
and the Elizabethans, including Shakespeare, in England.
From then on there is nothing except the refinements of
the eighteenth century, the romantic flowering, the mis-
takes of the bourgeois theatre and of the theatre "of
ideas." About the bourgeois theatre Ghéon said, "It renounces 'style' in the full sense of the word. To it, style
is lying, deceitful, an insult to reality; we must accept
the formless, honor and deify it as the only means of
expression." And about naturalism generally: ". . . there
was some recovery of the natural, some further loss of
style, or rather a final loss of style. By what door could
style re-enter, style that springs from poetry?"

Three French authors, however, rise above this morass,
in Ghéon's eyes. They are Alfred de Musset, Alfred Jarry
somewhat later, and finally Paul Claudel. Ghéon calls
Musset "A French Shakespeare brushed with Watteau's
wings!" But his liking for Alfred Jarry is significant; the
"hénaurme" (énorme) comic vocabulary of Jarry's *Ubu
Roi,* his satirical wit and his vitality delight and stimulate
Ghéon, who talks about "The presentation of *Ubu Roi,*
received as it was with a chorus of whistles, hisses, protests, and jeers—I was there myself." It is understandable: in Ghéon himself, in his own genius, there was

some touch of Jarry and of Ubu. And finally, Claudel. Though Ghéon first acknowledges the excesses of which Claudel the dramatist is guilty— "In him we see an acute conflict between practical playright and poet—each in turn using and abusing the other"—later on he pays him the highest respect: ". . . this is indeed the return of *style* to stage dialogue. . . . He is in the line of Aeschylus, Shakespeare, Calderón. . . ." But Claudel intimidates Ghéon: "We must be content to work humbly in his shadow." The humility is certainly sincere, but carries with it a feeling of removal, of distance. On the main point, however, Ghéon has seen clearly: since his death, Claudel's stage success has increased greatly.

To be sure, there are gaps in Ghéon's *Art of the Theatre*. The doctrine is a bit narrow, and at the same time the historical perspectives are incomplete. Leaving naturalism aside, it does not seem reasonable to overlook the contributions of modern realism. Ghéon mentions neither the Russian theatre nor certain features of Italian realism; Gogol, Chekhov, and Pirandello are passed over in silence. But even so, we cannot condemn the writer who has forewarned us (page 63) that "My ideas are not only incomplete but deliberately partial."

The very limits Ghéon set for himself give him a unique strength. I will always remember that it was he who convinced me that between the sixteenth and seventeenth centuries French dramatic art lost its universality; and it was he who helped direct my attention so vividly to Shakespeare and the Greeks.

Ghéon strayed more and more away from the time in which he lived. But he was too wise and too vital a man not to have a sense of the promises with which our torn age is pregnant. "Never perhaps in any other age, even the most fruitful, has so much talent been spent on dramatic art, in fact, on all the arts."

1960

MICHEL SAINT-DENIS

Translated by Robert Chapman

THE ART OF THE THEATRE

1:   CONDITIONS OF DRAMATIC ART

I AM going to talk to you about my favorite theories, my own thoughts about the theatre. They won't be anything new; they have grown out of the thoughts of many men. The only value thought has is to belong to the common tradition, to prolong it, to carry on that great spiritual continuity that links us still to our very sources. In all ages the masters were once disciples; receptivity is no hindrance to bold innovation. Good students do not necessarily become great masters, but at least they have the chance.

One reservation: I shall speak of the theatre only as a playwright and a director. My whole life has been dedicated to the writing and production of plays. Aside from my religion, this has been the center of my deepest thought and concern. I shall try now to focus these thoughts for you. The professional critic from his seat on the aisle may well disagree with me. True, he can see what escapes me; but I speak of what I know, and know from experience, as no critic can. If our viewpoints conflict, they may also complement each other.

What is dramatic art in its traditional form? *What* has it become? What *should* it become, what do we hope it

I

may become? I shall speak on these three points. My words may not convince all, but they may perhaps open the way to men of greater genius.

I

Let us first lay down some principles. Today for lack of guiding principles much good will, talent, even genius goes to waste; self-flattery, self-conceit, and self-preservation dominate all man's activities and especially literature and the arts. Even if it means being labeled dogmatic or pedantic, we must state boldly any truth we find of value. To drift aimlessly to and fro in the equivocal is the surest way to get nowhere.

Theatre is an *art*. Let us recall briefly the fact that art has two aspects: absolute and relative. It must be absolute: that is demanded by its very nature. An art that does not tend to the absolute, denies itself. Art is born in the mind and nowhere else; it is the ideal, the idea. Yet for all its philosophical and transcendental affinities, art is also relative because it is a technique, a craft that exists only in so far as it is practiced. If the work of art does not emerge from the mind to take perceptible form, it remains unfulfilled. The idea can be judged only by its execution, the genius only by his work. We have all dreamed marvelous poems that will never exist—because they remain a dream. That is the paradox: absolute in theory, art is relative in actuality; execution imposes on it conditions that are inevitably relative—relative to man, to his limitations, to his needs, to his means. That is what the Scholastics teach us, i.e., Aristotle as interpreted by Saint Thomas. It does not seem to me that, in aesthetics at least, we can reject their general conclusions. These conclusions, formulated in a subtle and profound little book, *Art and Scholasticism*, by Jacques Maritain, are exactly what experience teaches; they are not only the wisdom of the ages but also plain common sense.

"All art is free . . . and as art, it is disinterested. . . . The virtue of art looks only at one thing: the goodness to be created, the beauty to shine out from matter, to come into existence according to its own laws, independent of all else." Yet this theoretically pure art must meet something foreign, something opposed to itself, i.e., its instrument, its material. The art is in the artist, the artist in the man. "If there is no man, there is no artist"—and consequently no art. The man who wishes to create will meet a double resistance: the resistance of his own limited nature unable to subject itself wholly to what the mind demands; and the resistance of matter—the indocility of color, marble, sound, or word. He must compromise, he must also use violence; but if he goes too far, forcing the instrument to a note beyond its range, forcing matter into a form alien to its nature, then the instrument, matter itself, will take its own revenge. By all means let art tend to the maximum of freedom, to the absolute; such is its duty. But this maximum has a limit; beyond that limit lie meaninglessness, deformity, cacophony.

In a truly human and therefore relative aesthetic, it would be possible to classify the arts by that degree of the absolute to which they attain, and consequently by the sum of external factors which restrict them. On what level of this hierarchy is dramatic art?

Since Richard Wagner's ambition to restore the Greek tragic poets' concept of drama in "total theatre," such "total theatre" has been exalted as the shrine sacred to the meeting, the marriage, the fusion of all the arts. I do not deny that this point of view has its legitimacy and its grandeur. It is a fact that theatre alone can at one and the same time delight eye and ear and heart in a balanced harmony of plastic movement, music, and poetry.

Does, then, a union of all the arts necessarily produce a super-art? If they are truly united, yes.

Does it produce a purer art? Certainly not.

Each art sharing in this ideal synthesis under an expert hand must look to the other arts for support, inspiration, *élan,* emphasis: gesture must accentuate word, music prolong voice. Nowhere else are so many means available . . . not to mention the chief instrument—the living man, the actor, in whose spirit and flesh the work is given form and movement. But the more complex the material, the greater its resistance to one who seeks to mold it. As the means multiply, so do the servitudes. The result is that "total dramatic art" just because of its great resources becomes in fact the most confused, the most contingent of all arts, impeded by the heaviest passive resistance, balked at every step by massive obstruction.

Does that mean that Aeschylus and Sophocles were not able to master their material, that their greatest achievements were perhaps only brilliant compromises? We cannot know: the major part of their performances —the music, the dance—is forever lost. However, there is no doubt that Wagner in seeking to follow them destroyed all equilibrium of the arts: one art alone, music, submerges the whole drama. In my opinion there is more balance in Gluck and Mozart, in Debussy and Monteverdi. But that is not our subject here; at the moment I had better not go into the question of "total drama."

I do not mean that music ought never to be used to illuminate or to emphasize, but that it must always be as accompaniment, as relief or as interlude and no more. However, my subject here is literary drama in the form in which it has come down to us and is in actual use today: *the spoken drama.* Does that change the terms of our problem? No, for there is no theatrical art, however stylistic, abstract, intellectual, that does not participate in the other arts, that does not speak through eyes and ears to mind and heart, and that therefore does not demand of the playwright not only concern for good writing—a demand made equally on essayist, poet, novelist—but also an ear for musical order (rhythm, intonation), and an eye for plastic order (movement, image). We find here, then, the same contingencies as in "total drama," the same servitudes, the same "impurity." We must admit this honestly and try to work out a healthy dramaturgy; but first let us look at the causes for the sterility of modern theatre; i.e., our book-centered approach to drama.

II

There is some excuse for this long misunderstanding of the first principles of drama. Where could we learn save from books? The works of great playwrights survive only in the writings that record them. And as they come to us in the most abstract form, we are tempted to look on them as we do on masterpieces of poetry and fiction. Are they not only one more literary form among all the others—comedies of Aristophanes and tragedies of Sophocles, blood brothers to the *Eclogues* of Virgil and the *Dialogues* of Plato? Creon speaks to Antigone as Tityrus to Meliboeus, as Socrates to Alcibiades, though with perhaps a little more pathos. As we read, the drama takes shape in our head. But the laws that shape this drama hold good only for production inside our head and not outside it. Such imaginations are as far from the dramatic truth as the inner world is from the outer world. Don't imagine you have been present in spirit at the authentic drama of Aeschylus or of Shakespeare as Aeschylus and Shakespeare conceived it.

For neither Aeschylus nor Shakespeare, nor Sophocles, nor Calderón wrote plays for us *to read;* they wrote plays *to be acted on the stage* and on a *special* stage, plays for an audience and a special audience, plays for immediate production, immediate and evanescent. A few centuries later, even with the most reliable tradition and incontestable documents, we cannot even begin to imagine the way in which Champmeslé or Duparc interpreted Racine.[2] The most skillful revivals are and can be nothing more than adaptations. What relation is there between the original *Antigone* of the theatre of Dionysus and the academic *Antigone* of the Comédie-Française, even when revived by the genius of Mounet-Sully and Julia Bartet?[3] What the true *Antigone* was, we will never know, nor the *Passion* of Gréban,[4] nor *Othello,* nor *Phaedra,* nor *The Misanthrope.* All we have left is a dead book, a text, a skeleton, a blueprint; admirable as this may be, it is not the total living pattern created by those who conceived it and gave it life. The theatre has joined the "classics" in textbooks and lectures, for the esoteric pleasure of a few highbrows: it has become "literature." It is true that the highest form of theatre does deserve a place among literary forms, yet, I repeat, it is a unique literary form that curiously escapes from the printed page. If it does not overflow the page, it does not really exist at all, it has lost its own reason for existence, or if you prefer, has only a semiexistence. Like oratory, it leads a double life, in books and out of books. It would sacrifice the former rather than the latter, give up the library rather than the stage. We may study it in texts, but the text is only a fragment.

I do not deny its importance. It is the kernel, the mother cell, and nothing can replace it. "In the beginning was the Word . . ."—and this has universal validity. When thought renounces the word, it renounces its own definition; and to drive thought from the theatre would be to empty the theatre of substance, to degrade it. But granted that, we must also hold that drama has its own thought which is not that of poetry or of the novel, thought that must escape the written word if it is to have any life or power.

Book-life is enough for a poem, at least as poetry is conceived today—unfortunately perhaps—less and less for recitation and reading aloud, more and more for the silent, intimate joy of a solitary reader, a secret delight and song, murmured deep in the heart. Some even hold that no audience is needed at all, but this is extreme, monstrous—for the *sine qua non* of all art is to be communicable. Without going that far, let us say that, once recorded in a book, a poem can wait for its reader. We all know that Stendhal wrote his novels for readers to come a half-century after his death. Any purely literary work is almost completely achieved in its book, subject only to contingencies of grammar, logic, and, for poetry, of prosody. More or less beautiful typography changes nothing in the intrinsic value of the words as signs of things or of thoughts.

The playwright who thinks only in the written word as does a poet or novelist, who shapes beautiful forms vibrant with book-contained life, runs the risk of creating museum pieces, lifeless and incapable of life, with no momentum beyond the printed page. Of course, there is such a thing as an "armchair theatre" for those with enough imagination, and plays for such readers do exist, though they are really dialogue-novels. This is an essentially falsifying makeshift, one that hampered the career of the most genuine and perhaps the only truly dramatic writer of the nineteenth century, Alfred de Musset.

Another indefensible attitude is that of the playwright who polishes his sentences and hands them over to the director saying: "Here it is—I've done the words, the rest is your job." The words may be there, but they do not yet exist. Could an author who thus abandons his play once written, fancying that the text is enough, ever have put into that text what his art demands? Could he ever have charged the words with that power potential that alone makes them words of drama, dynamic, expressive, explosive? If so, would he not have wanted to make them come to life himself?

The word indeed rules all things, in the theatre as in books; it is the spirit's ambassador. But in the theatre it must be uttered by a human mouth, it must be incarnate in beings of flesh, it must live and move in them; it dictates the act and is the act (the *act* not in a Thomistic sense, but in the mechanical sense of movement). Before it touches and possesses the hearer, it must touch and possess a composite, indocile, and rebellious instrument: the stage, this particular concrete stage, with all its resources and all its resistances. When the playwright has trapped in written words the always relative absolute of his vision, that dream-group of personalities who meet, love, hate, live, and die at his good pleasure— he has as yet done nothing. He owes it to his art and to himself to design a dream that is realizable, viable, playable, and, if I may coin a pretty poor word, "exterioriza-ble." I repeat, he must not say, "Here are words, give them life, form, gesture, movement, action!" If that were enough, a scenario would do and drama would amount to no more than that embryo called *commedia dell'arte*. His very words must of themselves evoke image, gesture, movement, action, life; to add all this afterward is a poor artifice. Not that he must calculate them all ahead of time with implacable precision, leaving no room for the actor's imagination: this would paralyze the play. The life he must infuse is an appeal to the living actor; it calls out to another life, to life itself for its own accent and intonation. The playwright implicitly suggests to the interpreter a series of possibilities among which he need only choose. The playwright gives hints, fragments; the interpreter must put them together, give them sense.

But such foresight supposes that the author has complete grasp of technique. Even if he has an inborn feeling for the stage—he'll never write a play unless he has that —even so he must acquire its techniques humbly and perseveringly. Experience is indispensable. The stage offers itself to him as clay to the potter, stone or wood to the carver. Perhaps he will be tempted to take a part himself. . . . If he can, he should; then he truly be-comes master craftsman, master of the work. Who should be that master, if not the one who has conceived it? A Shakespeare, a Molière—author, director, and actor—that is the complete playwright.

Here you will quote my own words against me: "That is to canonize the ephemeral, the impermanent." This is exactly our difficulty. For posterity, the writer alone survives, as the material conditions of dramatic art are ever changing with the times. But my point is this: the dramatic writer does not write only for posterity, and to my way of thinking, he'll never reach it at all unless he first writes for his own time. I do not say that he should not seek to be a good writer; I mean that he must accept and embrace what is most transitory in his art, the only substances he can grasp, essentially evanescent as they are. I say that it is in them alone that he will make his drama a reality. I say that only in using them, with all their plus and minus qualities, their possibilities and their limitations, will he create a living thing, dramatically speaking. I say it is only at this price that after one century or ten, when nothing remains of his work but the words, those words will still keep a little of the dynamic power proper to drama and to drama alone. For if today we cannot revive the original *Antigone*, or the original *Macbeth*, or even the original *Polyeucte*, nevertheless they still have power to move us, fragmentary and changed though they may be; and they can move us in a way that no *Aeneid* or *Divine Comedy*, no *Don Quixote* or Platonic *Dialogue* can. Had the plays been conceived and executed in the abstract, they would perhaps have beauty, but another kind of beauty. The profound life hidden within them, still welling up within them, springs from their vital origin, for in their own day they were conceived in terms of living elements, they were lived out on a stage by men of flesh and bone. Written words, they were written for men's voices, for their masks and their bodies, and the words are still impregnated with this memory. Given such conditions, the play will be what it should be: a drama. Suppress this need of the playwright for immediate concrete realization and he loses his true being; he had better get another job.

There is nothing equal to the stage as a school for humility. The author is essentially dependent: dependent on the possibilities of the stage, dependent on the possibilities of the actor. In accord with the style, with the laws of the dramatic action (plastic form, movement, development), he must further appeal to the costumer, the set designer, the electrician, the mechanic, the director—if he does not himself direct—above all, to the actors. I should insist here on the harm done to dramatic art when the perilous harmony of these instruments is shattered, when the inadequacy of the play, of the playwright's skill, tempts one or another—director, designer, actor—to work on his own. That is the reason for the too-frequent failures in our contemporary theatre. . . . Do we then conclude that when the spirit of the play has fused author and actors into a living whole and the curtain goes up, then at last the work has come to life? . . . No, not at all—as yet, nothing has been done: there has to be an audience.

For dramatic art is not achieved by an author writing his play in a corner, nor by a group of trained actors giving it life on the stage; it requires also an audience to

receive it. It is author, actors, audience. We cannot eliminate any one of these three elements: they are integrally
bound together.[5]

You can imagine a picture that an artist paints for
himself alone. You can imagine a poem that the poet
recites to himself from morning to night but never re-
peats to other men. You can imagine a novel that has
never been read, asleep in a desk drawer. But you cannot imagine a play, written, rehearsed, staged, finally
produced, and then acted before empty chairs. At least
when this does happen, it is far from pleasing to actors
and author; for a play is not an end in itself. I mentioned above the strange liberty of novelist and poet in
regard to their public. In our time this has turned into
contempt for the public. It is true that to run after the
public, to flatter its prejudices and weaknesses, is not
the best way for an author to deepen and perfect his art.
But it is quite another thing to despise the public, to dis-
courage it, to slam the door in its face and refuse to
speak to it. The writer who seeks publication wants to be
read, otherwise he would write only to give form to his
own ideas, his dreams; no need to go into print. All art
is essentially social. But as I have also said, he who writes
books is absolutely free to wait for his public. They may
come or not, many of them or few, today, tomorrow, in
ten years or in a century. It does not matter. The poem,
novel, essay, remains printed on the pages of its book; it
exists now and will not exist with any more reality on the
day when it has ten thousand, twenty thousand, a hundred thousand readers. It is not influenced by the even-
tual reader; he cannot change it either before or after

(I am not speaking of commercial literature); it is the reader alone who is influenced, more or less deeply, sooner or later. Great writers, like our classic writers, will show a certain elementary and courteous consideration for their public, being careful in grammar, syntax, logic, using language not too remote from common speech. But they know too that a book can be reread, picked up when one wishes, put aside again, returned to, opened and closed again; hence they will not dilute their thought because it is difficult, nor their style because it is elliptical. If the reader complains, so much the worse for him—he is not worthy to understand! No poem or novel or essay need be popular.

The case is quite different with a dramatic work. It is like a book that is being read aloud, its pages turned remorselessly from the first to the last chapter. When a word has been spoken, it has been spoken; you cannot ask the actor to repeat it. That certainly would be a rich comedy, if you could imagine a difficult play punctuated by spectators rising in turn, demanding a replay of some fragment of the first act, a monologue in the third—they had missed the point at the time. The more intelligent —and those longing to seem intelligent—would protest with indignant "shushes!" Altercations, disorder, fist-fights! The drama would move off the stage into the house: action on the stage would stop. I am not fooling. Whether he pays for his seat or not, the spectator wants to understand, right on the spot, what the actor is saying. Hence the need of clarity, of intelligibility. The theatre is the very shrine of the manifest. This is the first servitude that the playwright must accept, willingly or not:

no matter how exquisite, stylized, erudite, significant, image-flowered it may be, the language he uses must be understandable by all.

A second servitude is no less rigorous. We must go beyond the letter and the word to the object which they signify. It is no use for the words to be exact, the sentences well constructed, the ideas logically and clearly developed, if the thought or feeling touches no chord in the minds and hearts of the audience and calls forth not even a faint echo of that feeling and that thought! Still worse if they call out a contrary reaction. That can happen; in fact it happens frequently. Some weep, and others laugh at the same thing; two plays are being performed at the same time, one comic, one pathetic. Which is the true play, tell me? The one the author intended? In that case, let him keep it to himself. He is expressing feeling and thoughts to his contemporaries that they do not share. "Excuse me," you may object, "do any two men ever have even one emotion or one idea exactly alike?" Certainly not, in details. But in general, yes. For there are certain intellectual and moral values on which the majority agree in any real society: good and evil, true and false (I do not say beauty and ugliness; these are aesthetic values, and as such are subject to variation in the best of societies; let us not get involved in pure aesthetics, please). Agreement on what is good, agreement on what is true: the man who writes for the theatre must create at least that minimum of communion between his work and his audience. Only then will he touch feelings and win the assent he desires. A play exists, really exists, lives and really lives, only when its life-spark leaps from the stage and from the playwright's soul across to the audience in a moment of vital contact. That is why Jacques Copeau said in a phrase I love to quote:

There will never be a new theatre (meaning a reaction against today's falsified theatre in a return to tradition) until the day comes when the man in the audience murmurs in his heart and with his heart the same words spoken by the man on the stage.

Yes, the day when author and spectator—and, I may add, actor also, for he is the hyphen between them—are one, and stand together on the same intellectual and moral ground. For communion we need such ground. But it can exist only in a truly organic society, by which I mean a society that has a center, a coherence and unanimity: it recognizes one good as *good* and one truth as *true*.

But if society is not organic, or if there is no society at all—what happens? Well, there will not be any theatre, or at the most a fragmentary, stammering, time-serving theatre. There will be no understanding, no communication, no communion. The play will have to crawl into the book, and wait for better days.

It cannot wait too long; for in the theatre, too long a delay in realization alters the concept itself. While the author is working on his play, unless he has at hand and under his control all the elements of language and technique as well as actors and audience, the validity of his "creative activity," as Maritain says, will be hopelessly falsified. He is not one, but two, or rather three; what matters is not only that many speak in his name, but that all should answer him.

There is a school that conceives the stage as a room with one wall removed where something happens. I imagine it more as a platform set up in the midst of a crowd, a place of perpetual barter. A dramatic author must make a practical study of the conditions of that barter, discover its laws, make sure that it is possible, that he is not speaking a tongue alien to his public.

Thus dramatic art presupposes both in theory and in fact the existence of a homogeneous society, a "people" in the noblest meaning of the word. It is not a closed art, nor a long-range art, but an open, immediate art. Pity the author who feels within himself power to give substance to a dream that haunts him, yet who can find nothing outside to help him. It would be a miracle if he could create life in the present only by his hope for the future. True, there are certain great works that for special reasons did not succeed in their author's lifetime, even though they were essentially in accord with their age; their dramatic success was only a little deferred. But no plays of real vitality were misunderstood and rejected in their own day only to grip the emotions of an audience centuries later. Plays that survive or revive, as I have said, are plays that have once been alive.

Such are the essential conditions for drama. It depends on its own lifetime to exist or not. No talent, not even genius is enough: good luck is needed too.

You understand that all these principles call for qualification. There are special cases that escape the general rule and to which I shall return. The important thing is that the problem be established on solid ground. I take back nothing essential. The born dramatist may also be a great poet or a great creator of characters; his art may embrace beauties that poetry and novels can possess only fragmentarily, for being neither poet nor novelist, he can call a whole world into life and movement. Yet by this very fact he must work in a relative medium with substance that is in part perishable. No withdrawal to his tower will safeguard purity. Unless he comes down again, the work will not be a play. The dramatist is imprisoned in the contingencies of theatre and of society; the character of his art is essentially social.

Having made that clear, I shall next outline the changing destiny of the playwright down through the centuries, and discover what he can hope for, subject as he is to harsh necessities, in the world of today—and of tomorrow.

2: From the Origins to the Classical Age

WE HAVE seen what makes dramatic art a unique literary genre: the most all-embracing and complex yet also the most abjectly enslaved, the high point of sublimity and of confusion, a literary genre that to be truly itself must cease to be literary.

It needs author, actors, audience. A play is born in time, at a certain moment of time, for that time alone and not for any other. It can and even must desire to survive, but its future depends on the vigor of its present.

By nature it is *action,* and if the author has not tested its acting power on the stage and on an audience, it remains mere potentiality—as insubstantial as the dream of a picture never painted or of a statue never carved in wood or stone.

Dramatic art is an art of barter, of interchange; dramatic art is a social art. Therefore it grows from religion. *Religio*: that which binds; the strongest bond of society.

I

The tragedy of Aeschylus was an act of worship. On a festival day, before the assembly of a whole people for whom the gods were truly their Gods, the heroes truly their heroes, the founders truly their guardians, the ever-present protectors of their city, the *Fasti* of their local history were re-enacted. The people relived great deeds of those gods and heroes, the crimes and sufferings of their own kin under the law of Destiny: Prometheus bound to his rock, his body torn by the vulture, his spirit rent with defiance; Troy and its fall; the dreadful banquet of Atreus with its sequel of inherited guilt and divine mercy; even the recent victory over the Persians, still a living memory.

These themes were popular, they were the very substance of the people themselves. The work of the tragic poets was to exalt with great dignity the common thought, the common faith. The poet's work was offered to the people; the people themselves crowned the winner, that poet at whose words their hearts felt again the passion of Prometheus, of Oedipus, of Orestes; the poet who for a day had given living flesh again to those great ghosts.

Then Comedy was born. At first it was wholly political, scandalously frank about daily events, boldly attacking the great and the powerful by name. Later with Menander in Greece, Plautus and Terence in Rome, it dealt with more generalized types: the Miser, the Boaster, the Parasite. The contact was not yet broken, as long as Plautus still spoke to the people in their own language and still set up his platform in the midst of the crowd, playing in the public squares like the very early farces. But like Euripides' tragedy, so the comedy of Menander and Terence developed into a closed and specialized art intended only for the discriminating few. These poets in fact killed off the original drama; after them it no longer existed. Seneca read his tragedies to a select audience; were they ever acted? Deprived of its natural aids, without actor or audience, the theatre had petered out. It now became literature, a literature that was nothing to boast of.

The curve of dramatic art from the late Middle Ages to our own day is no less significant. It was born again from worship, from Christian liturgy. The Mass, the central act of worship, is essentially a drama: for the faithful it is the drama of dramas, the real drama in which the Son of God in person participates each morning. To honor and to express this profound reality, no exterior magnificence or grace is too much, every movement of the celebrant, of the deacons, of the acolytes, the singing of the choir, the response of the whole congregation—all is regulated and significant. The theatre properly so-called had only to amplify the liturgical set-up, to make the teaching of the Word more direct, its secret reality more perceptible. One day some clerics got the idea of impersonating the Theological and Cardinal Virtues before the altar; of representing Moses, Isaiah, all the prophets of the coming of Christ by a solemn procession in rich vestments; then of dramatizing the parables: the Wise and Foolish Virgins with their lamps waiting for the Bridegroom. Soon they were acting the life of the Son of God, then the life and miracles of the Blessed Virgin, then the miracles of our saints. But the plays by then had left the sanctuary for the town square where brilliantly decorated platforms graphically presented Earth, Heaven, and Hell, the whole temporal and spiritual universe, the triple Church of

Christian dogma. The spectators, even the indifferent, even the unworthy, accepted these fictions with as much faith and certitude as the reality they represented. The scope of the productions, the spontaneous and unanimous response they found in the people, are proof that this was indeed total drama.

So the Mystery plays and Miracle plays were born. They were familiar, popular, easy to understand, at times broadly farcical, even degenerating into irreverent buffoonery, which later led to the intervention of the secular arm. These plays flourished as a genre for three centuries, a genre from which sprang the Corneille of *Polyeucte,* the Molière of *The Doctor in Spite of Himself,* expressing the whole life of French society with all its native cheerfulness, its common sense, its virtues and vices, its good and bad qualities—and its faith. For even when man himself became the Miracle play's chief interest, the saints, especially Our Lady, would always intervene in the end.

The secular theatre came into being at the same time and with the same spirit in various places, under the form of little plays and farces. It was always social and popular, for a pre-established harmony on basic unassailable moral values reigned between the play and the public. Anyone could come to the play—and everyone would find something to suit himself; for there was poetry and sometimes music too. The actors of these little plays were the common people, belonging to *Confraternities* which professional mountebanks did not enter.

Did these medieval Mystery plays then, from primitives

like Rutebeuf to flamboyants like Gréban, all achieve perfection of theatrical form in a total dramatic art? The answer is no. Even including the early *Miracle of Théophile* and the late *Passion* of Gréban and of Jean Michel,[6] I find no real masterpiece, only fragments of masterpieces. There was not time to reach maturity. No doubt the Mystery was an impressive spectacle, beyond our power to imagine today, with its processions, singing, interludes of every kind. But with all the vivid impact of those charming, animated, rich scenes that delight us still, defects leap out when we read these plays, defects only more obvious on the stage: endless repetition, useless detail, prolixity, never getting anywhere, lack of discrimination between the essential and the accessory. There is no pattern, no design, only a succession of often unrelated tableaux more or less skillfully linked together, with no progression, no build-up to crises and the resolution of the crises, no gradation of effect. Although these Mysteries went on for several days, not only was there no consecutive pattern for the whole series, but not even one day was a unified and consistent whole, as the trilogy in Greek drama allowed. Hence the effect would be very strange to us, formed as we are by the tradition of the Greek theatre. The medieval dramatists lacked maturity both in language and in dramatic craftsmanship: they have left us drama in embryo only. But with genius and talent (there was true genius among them), with attention to technique, with the study of ancient drama rediscovered by the Renaissance, that childish art could have attained true maturity since it enjoyed the uniquely favorable environment of a true society, one

in heart. It already contained all the unorganized yet
authentic elements of the most genuine French tradition:
it was Christian, it was human, it was cheerful and
chivalrous, it could pray and weep, it could laugh, in
harmony not only with its own times but with the
French people as they are even today—if you scratch a
little below the surface: our peasants, our workers, our
middle class, and even—with a little harder scratching—
our intellectuals: do we not possess Charles Péguy? [7] The
voice of France was there. Never was such wealth of
national material offered to any author.

II

But at that moment the Reformation cut Christianity
in two and the pagan Renaissance moved north from
Italy. It brought invaluable treasures to add to our own,
but treasures which proved almost overpowering. The
French mind has since had to grapple with material
which, though not alien—the Graeco-Latin tradition had
inspired our Middle Ages—was not yet at home, not yet
Christian and French. The assimilation of this material
to France and Christianity was the work of the seventeenth century. An idea of art then matured that intoxi-
cated the artist with self-love; he found himself master
of a new and exclusive kingdom. He was no longer an
artisan among others and, as Du Bellay confessed, grew
ever more contemptuous of the "judgment of the boorish
common folk"—that judgment so powerful to rectify the
errors and moderate the excesses of individual judgment.
This *coup d'état* of the elite did not harm book literature,
but the contemporary theatre died of it. At least it was
one cause of that death. The sixteenth century offered

the French common people a pale copy of Hellenistic tragedy.

I do not make any accusations; facts cannot be accused, especially as the next century drew from these same new treasures new material and new methods for great achievements. I only regret that this religious and social upheaval cut off the development of a truly French theatre that had needed only to be perfected technically and aesthetically. The resurrection of the Greek theatre attempted by the *Pléiade* was a failure: Jodelle[8] achieved nothing great. Some Protestant writers, the most remarkable of whom was Louis des Masures, produced powerful scenes of Biblical tragedy, in an art derived from the Mysteries, yet they were not popular.[9] The spirit of chivalry survived for some time through Spanish influence among Corneille's precursors. Only in Spain and England did the medieval drama take new life and bear its noble fruit: the greatest medieval dramatist is Shakespeare.

I know, of course, how much the Elizabethans owe to antiquity through Renaissance humanism. Their sources include the *Essays* of Montaigne and the *Plutarch* of Amyot, nor may we forget Seneca: they knew the Greeks only through his dark distortions that gave them their taste for horrors. Yet under the sixteenth-century varnish still breathed the medieval man: Christian, gallant, and violent. With a few exceptions, the Elizabethan drama was a popular drama, akin to the spirit of the people among whom it was born. Remember that in the time of Henry VIII and Elizabeth, the Reformation had not touched the substance of dogma, save the supremacy of Peter; it was still a schism, political in origin and in character. Before the Puritan attack split it into innumerable sects, English Christianity was unchanged in spirit, keeping all the Roman Catholic rites. Shakespeare wrote his plays, or most of them, for that Anglo-Christian world. Like his medieval ancestors and ours, he found it natural to mingle farce and tragedy.

In his greatest works, comic interludes, burlesques, obscenities, designed to hold the attention even of the Thames dockhands, are followed the next moment by exquisite poetry whose welling stream enchants the most fastidious taste. Aside from the enigmatic *Hamlet* whose depths probably conceal a void rather than a mystery, all his dramas are clearly constructed on a moral pattern —I do not say moralizing—a pattern that is Christian and even Catholic. He shows us no criminal escaping punishment, no courtesan sentimentalized, no evil action interpreted as good: people who believe in good and evil understand him perfectly. And, finally, he conceives drama in the medieval manner, as a succession of scenes that carry us from place to place. His mature genius eliminated the medieval trivialities; everything is functional and the more serious the conflict, the deeper the pathos. He handles comedy too with sovereign freedom. He does not eliminate secondary actions but subordinates them; the accessory never distracts from the essential. Not that his mechanics of plot attain the austerity we admire in Racine. He designed in patterns of successive movement, with all the diverse elements ever moving toward patterned order, an order that is almost always achieved. If we could transpose his art into the language and spirit of France, we would have what the medieval

French theatre might have become, had it been allowed to develop without brutal dislocation into a drama which, although literary, was always open to the people, open in every way to all.

This can be said also of the great Spanish drama of Tirso de Molina, Lope de Vega, Calderón.[10] The harsh religion of Spain, rebelling against the novelties of the Reform and the rebirth of paganism, willed to create an essentially religious and Catholic theatre. This Catholicism is not always ours; it often shocks us. The doctrine behind the *Devotion to the Cross* or the *Damned for Lack of Confidence,* for example, seems scandalous to us, although some of our own Mysteries make equally explicit statements: the brigand is saved by a precarious act of faith, the saint damned for a moment's disbelief. Other times, other customs. The Spanish plays were not written for us. But they do correspond to the Iberian temperament; there are no others so autochthonous, less influenced by foreign elements, and they achieve universality just because they keep all the substance of their nation's life-blood. We ourselves have seen the success of the great play, *Life is a Dream,* in the theatre of the Paris Atelier. Spain had comedy too, running riot with intrigue, comedy which inspired Corneille. But in the special and strictly confessional form of the feast day *Autos Sacramentales,*[11] acted on floats in the squares, Spanish drama plunged still deeper into the life of the people, into the Catholicism from which that life sprang. Mystical and cruel, originally very remote from our old Mysteries, yet it is built on the same foundations of fatherland and of faith.

Where does our classical drama part from those foundations, even when inspired by them, as in *The Cid*, *The Liar*, the *Don Juan* of Molière? Is this beloved art of ours opposed to all that went before it? Is it the beginning of the "closed theatre"?

My friend René Salomé has made a remarkable study of the emergence of a closed theatre in opposition to the primitive theatre, national or religious and, in general, popular; a new theatre reserved for the elite, with no welcome for a chance spectator. This theatre provides the pleasures suited to refined and highbrow tastes; needle-pointed psychological analysis, or incredibly subtle poeticism, or *avant-garde* themes that pervert current intellectual or moral principles. The audiences would be very select—though snobbery adds to their numbers—and above any "prejudices" at all: moral, national, religious, or even human! All they have in common is pleasure in the peculiarity, the abnormality of the artistic acrobatic skill that enchants them. Yet do not conclude that even here the *sine qua non* of true dramatic art cannot be realized! There is in fact a basis for communion in the very intellectual appeal, the aesthetic novelty for which the spectator is prepared. It seems to me there is even an excess of communion. But I will speak of this later. Now I must return to my theme.

It is true, at least partially true, that the theatre of the seventeenth century suddenly ceased to be popular, in the wider sense of that word, to become almost exclusively and in the narrowest sense a class theatre. I will qualify this somewhat extreme statement in a moment. First, at least in tragedy, it eliminated as much as possible all that delights the eye. The charms of ornate scenic effects fled to musical theatre, to ballet and opera. Just how far the so-called rules of Aristotle contributed to the purification is very doubtful. His theory was usually quoted only to justify already existing practices or the secret current drawing minds in this direction. Calvinism, Jansenism, and later Cartesianism were in the main responsible, and their influence, added to an ever-sharpening curiosity about the psychology of the interior man, led our classical writers to give form to a hitherto undetermined art: the drama of man in his inmost substance.

We see then a bare stage, or almost bare, a set that never changes; Corneille himself gave up any scene shifts. The same limitation was then applied to time. Since the more the drama was restricted, the more emphasis and tragic power it achieved, pathos became its very essence; anything that might distract from this must be eliminated. That included all relief, diversion, fantasy, even poetry. The drama would take men at a moment of crisis, in the most acute moment of that crisis, to be revealed, intensified to a crescendo, and resolved, all between dawn and sunset. The Greeks did not go that far. Their minds were not so tormented with logic and they were able to avoid the pitfalls of plot intrigue. Narrow and rigid laws might give the play a strong skeleton, but also led to the artificial, mechanical conventionality which we find in the immediate and later followers of the great masters. Yet the masters used the laws to achieve an austerity, an intensity, a perfection of dramatic art unknown before and probably unsurpassable: Corneille in *Polyeucte,* Racine in *Britannicus*. Man is alone; he cannot speak to friend or enemy yet his words reveal everything. If a crime is committed, we will not see it: no matter, we will feel its presence. What interests us is less what man does than what happens within him: this is interior drama. But its interiority does not make it less dramatic. A smile of Monime or of Berenice, a cry of Polyeucte or of Phaedra, for which we have been prepared, is as overwhelming to us as the terrible apparition of Lady Macbeth trying in vain to wipe the blood from her hand. By "us" I mean the seventeenth-century gentleman, the man of letters, the lawyer, or the courtier. But what about the ordinary people? The majority of Frenchmen? Well, it was a theatre for the elite, granted: theatre for its own sake, first of all. Yet that is to say too little. It was for society too; I do not mean that it was conceived primarily for society, but at least it was not conceived as an attack upon it. For in fact it was wholly in harmony with it.

Our classical tragic poets, beginning with Racine, were too richly human, too balanced, ever to dream of freeing themselves from the universal conditions of their art. They may not have offered a mixed audience anything to captivate the senses—no brilliant spectacle, no scenes of murder, blows, clamor, and blood, but they did make their characters (aside from some clichés like their beloved *chains* or *flames of love*), speak a language that for all its polish was clear and direct; to hear was to understand. And ordinary people are never unresponsive to words. Moreover these words expressed no thoughts or feelings at variance with the common mentality. The pagan heroes of the plays may have been almost unknown to the common man, yet these heroes portrayed Christian values by which the masses still lived, as did almost all of French society, including even the "libertines." For we must note, and I am not the first to point this out, that even Racine poured into an antique mold a psychological content which had been elaborated by ten centuries of Christianity, while in Corneille the very spirit of chivalry survived its medieval framework. Phaedra knows the monstrous nature of her love and seeks to silence it; Nero, though hardened in evil, knows perfectly well that he is guilty of evil. In this world of high-flown heroics evil and good are still known for what they are and put where they belong. What, then, has the average man got to complain about? Finally, Racine's most thin-spun subtleties of analysis lead up to those great strokes of tragic synthesis that create before us the whole living person. Before "us"? This time, I mean "before the whole world."

"Wait, Nero, I have a word for you." [12] A vast audience, a whole theatre will tremble at these words.

But I must add that with Racine we have reached that point where the peril implicit in literary analysis ceases to be a threat: it has become a fact. Theatre that is too refined, too literary, is of necessity too remote from its object. Thanks to supreme common sense, the poet of *Andromache* kept his drama accessible to all. The tragic art of 1650, with its special conditions and problems, needed all that detachment, that introversion, to create those few, uniquely great plays. But to lean too much on the approval of the "pure," the elite who alone can perceive all the subtle nuances in a work that, objectively speaking, is simple and clear, is to risk the temptation of despising the common man, of writing only for that "pure" elite. Such is the fate of all "*cénacles*"; we have come here to the borderline between the theatre and the book.

We will never know how far Racine's dissociation of sentiment and consequently of personality would have gone, had not his secular work been interrupted by his conversion. The wider Biblical themes that he later handled imposed on him a more direct, elementary, and healthy aesthetic. He never lived to grow old. The old age of the great Corneille with its lightning flashes of genius, however, demonstrates the dangers of oversubtlety. Disquieted, perhaps jealous of the success of his young rival, he gave up painting in broad mass patterns, designing in great sweeps, and turned to cultivate by choice his very defects. Hence the artificiality, the inextricable intrigue and elliptical trickery that make most of his later tragedies almost unreadable and perhaps, alas, unplayable. His audiences made that only too clear to him. But the most striking proof of the crisis that beset classical drama on the morrow of its flowering is found in the true heir of Racine, the marvelous Marivaux.[13]

He took the step his master had not taken and no doubt had tried hard not to take: Marivaux wrote for himself alone. Please note that I enjoy Marivaux's art— both as literature and drama; but we must distinguish between the two. What captivated him was not human personality but exotic sentiments. In his desire to surprise himself and us with his ingenuity, he split hairs into fourths, eighths, sixteenths, thirty-seconds. No one declares himself until he has twenty times un-declared himself; no one loves until he has twenty times un-loved; no one gives himself save to take himself back and then give himself again—and in the end you don't know whether he is given or un-given. Sentiments play their own part in a subtle and transparent game. But through this delicate network the divided personality slips away, the man of flesh is effaced, dissolved. Nothing is left on the stage but a charming conversationalist, skillful in cutting capers and pirouettes—the only thread by which the play still holds on to dramatic art. This mechanism turns out nothing of substance, nothing but words. I challenge anyone to name a single character among all Marivaux's lovers and adventurous ladies. There is no Rodrigue, no Monime. One step more, and dramatic art is buried. At least, it is now at its own wake, its plays acted in subdued candlelight before a half dozen select guests.

IV

That is the closed theatre that has dominated the stage since Racine. Was the tradition of the open theatre lost at the very moment when dramatic art attained perfection?

No, one man kept it in existence, and with such energy and rough violence that even today his art appeals to the man in the street as much as to the elite, and perhaps even more. That man is Molière, and to the credit of his century we must recall that he was loved by the general public and supported by the king. For the elite of those days was not as cut off from the national community as historians claim. It was a cheerful elite; it understood healthy humor. It was not composed entirely of "les précieux"— what we call today the avant-garde. Molière was an anti-précieux, an anti-aesthete.

Molière came from the people, from a family of workers, lower-middle class, and in his farces, even in his comedy of manners, never lost touch with his origins. Boileau complains of the "bag that Scapin wraps around himself"; he is wrong to complain. By this bag Molière affirms and confirms the great synthetic tradition of true theatre that demands clearly defined objects, solid characters with bold outline, vividly visualized action. He insisted on the rights of exterior actions, graphic in gesture as well as in word.

In this gesture and action, the primal and essential power is rhythm. It is true that he owes much of this to the Italian farce, but his imitation is creation; his technique, poetry.

A parenthesis: to me the authentic Molière is the Molière of prose. Not that I dislike his verse, neither in the youthful *The School for Wives,* nor the mature *Misanthrope*, nor *Tartuffe*, with all its bitterness. But in these plays he seems hampered by literary constraints not meant for him. This criticism does not apply to the *Amphitryon* and to his part of the *Psyche,* which are miracles of varied ease. Yet had Molière never learned how to rhyme, he would have lost nothing. Even when the Alexandrine does not clash with his inborn personal rhythm, at least it moderates it, attenuates it, smooths down its angles, makes it less cutting, less convincing and less effectively graphic. Even when his verse is at its most felicitous, its most brilliant, equal to those marvelous tirades of *The Liar*,[14] he seems to be wearing a ready-made suit that does not fit. Only his good sense saves him from awkward gestures, embarrassed as he is by all that encumbers him. Whether he wrote his verse in contradiction or in humility, it is more prosaic than his prose, lacking his inspired inner rhythm.

Take any scene, for example, the first in *The Doctor in Spite of Himself!*

SGANARELLE: No, I tell you I won't have anything to do with it and I'm the one lays down the law—I'm master here.
MARTINE: And I tell you I'll make you live the way I please and I didn't marry you to put up with your nonsense.[15]

Péguy says of Corneille and Racine that their first words fall like an avalanche, thunderous, abrupt, a sudden plunge into the action, sweeping us along into its heart:

"Impatient desires for a glorious revenge . . ."

or

"Yes, since I have found so faithful a friend . . ."

or

"Yes, I come to His temple to adore the Eternal One" [16]

No one has had such success with this in prose as Molière. The accent, the rhythm, is there in the very first words: two compact, square, symmetrical phrases, each demanding bodily gesture, each boldly sketching a personality in full action. The movement is irresistible, sweeping on, full tempo, accelerating, slowing down, speeding up again. Sentences of equal length, stanzas, long parallel with long, short with short, followed by alternation of long and short:

MARTINE: I have four poor little babes in arms . . .
SGANARELLE: Put them down on the ground.
MARTINE: Crying to me pitifully all day long for bread . . .
SGANARELLE: Shut them up!

And the final "presto," the most brilliant in all comedy, which cascades its exclamations to end, plop! with a flat and flattening phrase, absolutely sure in its perfect balance:

MARTINE: You drunk!
SGANARELLE: I'll beat you up!
MARTINE: You beer can!
SGANARELLE: I'll give you a licking!
MARTINE: Tramp!
SGANARELLE: I'll comb you out!
MARTINE: Traitor, crook, coward, villain, pickpocket, gallows-bird, robber!
SGANARELLE (*raising stick*): Ah, so that's what you want? (*beating her*)
MARTINE: Oh! oh! oh! oh!
SGANARELLE: That's the only way to satisfy you.[17]

Is that prose? Whatever you call it, it belongs to the theatre and to the theatre only. The theatre needs prose like that, instead of the invertebrate dialogue we get today: a direct, vital, stylized prose that calls out, follows up and fuses with graphic action, generating impulse in rhythmic exchange. It is not always so biting, so swift, so insane. A slow movement of dialogue punctuated by silences obeys the same principles, produces the same varied effects. I know no clearer, more eloquent example of what the playwright's constructive thought should be. He must pattern not only feelings and ideas, but words and actions, the word bound to the action, the action to the word.

Molière thus creates close, continuous, living, organic contact with the audience by a linked sequence of apt words whose vivid impression of ordinary speech compels us to listen; by a linked sequence of actions that compels us to watch; by choreographic modulation of patterned movement that sweeps our whole being on toward the denouement. . . . Almost all Molière's prose comedies are conceived as ballets, dynamic and plastic as the dance. They are written to be danced to the music of the script, in a free and controlled improvisation where word and step alike spring up in harmony. You would have to be blind and deaf not to be carried away by this orchestration of sense-symbols, wedded to and expressing the playwright's secret thought.

That is what makes the art of farce essentially popular, above all when it expresses thoughts in accord with average good sense, and when its characters show the usual and foreseeable reactions of the moral code prevailing in daily life. There we see good men and bad, wise men and fools and plain idiots; in fact, we see life —the life of our time, of all time. We are at home, we recognize and understand ourselves. What are the conditions for such complete success? Genius by itself is not enough. Molière had also a theatre and a group of actors; Molière had an audience. He never had Racine's temptation to compose at his desk, writing to delight himself and a few beautiful minds; his actors and his audience were waiting for him. *He knew his actors;* he had organized the group, he knew what they could do. Every word, therefore, was written in function of a possible intonation, mime and gesture. He worked surely and feverishly in living substance. Feverishly? Certainly; a sense of urgency is a large part of the power of a play. It may be a long time ripening, it may later be polished with patient care; but it must be written with excitement. *He knew his audience*; he knew that it included the elite and the masses, the courtier and the man in the street; he wanted them all to understand him. He had studied the techniques that put over a word or a gesture; he knew the rhythm, volume, style, and feeling that would capture both elite and masses. Side by side with the *salons* in seventeenth-century France, thank God, there still existed a society in the wider sense of the word, and to this he belonged. He had no need to do violence to his own nature to be in tune with his time.

Yes, beside genius, he had luck and he had happiness: the happiness of being a practical man of the theatre, not a literary man; the happiness of having an instrument at hand, adapted to his own powers; the happiness of being in harmony with his time, with public opinion, with his audience. He gave himself to it with all his heart in complete confidence. There was nothing hybrid here: writer and producer were one. At no moment in his career did craftsmanship fail him, the "fabricating activity," as Thomists say. He had his own idea of art that creates from and in matter. Author, actor, and audience all collaborated in secret within him before collaborating in the open theatre.

Here, then, owing to Molière's all-embracing and direct communication and exchange, the tradition of the open theatre found new life. I have mentioned *The Liar*. Some comedies of Corneille, of Regnard (from one point of view, even those of Marivaux), and later those of Beaumarchais, linked as they were by the theatre of the market place,[18] all form a continuous chain leading back to that ancient tradition. Today we must return there.

But a new thing happened: a closed theatre had been

established for the elite, suggested, if not accomplished, by Racine. We must face this, for the nineteenth century produced strange hybrids of open and closed theatres. Would it not be better to separate them? Society has collapsed, and drama has decayed with it. To re-create dramatic art, must we re-create society?

3: From *Hernani* to the Théâtre Libre of Antoine

The genius of Molière saved comedy from the fate of tragedy, but its varying fortunes were for the most part inglorious—Beaumarchais is the exception. The tone, the style, and the survival of the comic playwright was due entirely to the father of comedy. Only three writers in the nineteenth century are worth mentioning: Labiche (yes, Labiche), Courteline, and Georges Feydeau.[19] But what happened to tragedy?

I

Racine's tragedy died of its own perfection. It survived only in Voltaire; the only masterpiece it produced was Goethe's *Iphigenia*, a closet drama, adapted to the little closed theatre of Weimar. In France the seventeenth-century vogue for Racine gradually yielded to a fashion for Corneille, whose more exteriorized tragic form was revived by the Revolution and the Empire, in the style of those periods. But in spite of the infusion of a few drops of Shakespearean blood, it became exclusively oratorical, stilted, affected—a matter of striking attitudes, of flowery speeches. David, master of the abstract style, established neoclassicism. His Graeco-Roman allegories

41

broke with the truly classical schools, although Chardin carried on the old French art and in Watteau the great Flemish tradition survived. David's mediocre imitators in the theatre, losing all contact with mankind, set before their audience only heroes of ice, or, rather, abstract virtues masquerading as heroes. The vulnerable Christian of the seventeenth century with his Greek or Roman name gave way to the impassive stoic. Idealization, intended (in what was incorrectly thought to be the Greek way) to make art more readable, more impressive, only dried it up. Movement was sacrificed to the statuesque, dynamism to a pseudo sublimity. These noble forms degenerated into a hollow formalism, an antihuman rhetoric. Tragedy had said its last word to the general public. By flattering the passions of the hour—it is riddled with political allusions—it produced the illusion of life. But when the political scene grew calm, there was nothing to keep tragedy alive.

Realistic bourgeois drama, the creation of Diderot, La Chaussée, Sedaine,[20] emerged as the only victor of this confused struggle, the insignificant heir to an art repudiated by its own mediocrity and for a whole century deprived of all poetry.

But let us not anticipate. The thunderous success of romantic drama is easy to explain, following as it did upon the reign of David. Everyone was tired of speeches and attitudes, of hearing about things instead of seeing them, for the pseudo classicists had none of Racine's power to suggest the presence of the unseen. Shakespeare was discovered and served up by Ducis[21] with soothing sauces poured over his crudities. Action and movement were demanded. They tried to transfer the direct art of

Molière and of Shakespeare into the five-act tragedy framework. But here the reformers disagreed: the poets, the men of letters, opposed the nonliterary men, the nonpoets. The age of democracy was beginning and the writers reflected its split society. Two forms of romantic drama appeared, perhaps related to each other, but never meeting.

The poetic and literary reform, especially that of the Hugo group, was theoretical in character. Hugo blamed the dessicated state of tragedy on the rules alone, yet at the same time kept the traditional Alexandrine and the plot mechanics invented by the enemy—Racine being the greatest villain among them all. Hugo's aim was to "purify" drama from all that was not violent and tragic. He did not see that Racine's tone of moderation, like Corneille's irony, was a comic technique to keep his feet on the ground, that his heroes might remain truly human, not taken in by their own nobility and pathos; that their despair and fury might have depth, tonality, shading, a kind of chiaroscuro. Instead, Hugo used black-and-white contrast, turning the antithesis into an aesthetic principle—the most stupid possible. Symbolic use of antithesis can be striking; but it is one thing to use it with respect for probability, and quite another to abuse it, outraging all common sense. We do not create life by setting its extreme elements at war with one another. This senseless aesthetic in fact was based on a war-minded ethic, a blind revolutionary will to overthrow the moral values on which the majority of Frenchmen at that time still agreed. In Hugo the criminal is always the noblest of men, the respectable man the most depraved; the valet has the soul of a great aristocrat, the prostitute, the abnegation of a saint. Such is life. . . . Nonsense. This is a party platform, with a pitifully meager ideology. Hugo thought to break with the classical artifice that had polarized certain emotions, pruning the complexity of the person but still respecting his essential truth; he only invented a new artifice to destroy truth itself. This defender of truth, this champion of man, worked in a closed little box, without contact, without real love. He was incapable of ever getting outside himself, of creating human character. Images? As many as you want, the latest and the most elaborate. Real beings? Not the shadow of one. Humanly speaking, I know nothing more abstract than the impoverished thought beneath his ornate and magnificent exuberance.

From all that, a pseudo-Shakespearean monster emerged: a tragedy without substance, a skillful framework braced up with words but empty of soul.

In any case, how could we expect any dramatic art from poetic romanticism, ever more and more concentrated on the ego? A romantic dreams only of himself, thinks only by himself, lives only for himself. He offers himself for the world to admire, refusing to risk going out into the world. His theatre, in fact, needs only an author; the actor doubles for him as passive instrument, serving him only, not the character. Why even have an actor? There are no more characters. Is there even an audience?

For a long time there was a public that enjoyed the drama of Victor Hugo. But I believe there was something dubious about that audience—the same that would later applaud Rostand's plays. It was in fact a victimized audience, flogged with verbiage, unable to distinguish

words from things; blinded by imagery, unable to discern
hallucination from reality; tricked by intrigue, hypno-
tized by language; and the conjuror gave it no moment's
respite to regain consciousness. A closed theatre for an
elite? No. Anyone with taste and reflection would have
been the first to abandon it. A popular theatre, then?
Perhaps, but in the worst sense of the word, a theatre in
which the author collaborates with the crowd by flattering it, blinding it, and deluding its good will. That is
what happened to the theatre of Henri Bataille, a too
sophisticated theatre.[22]

But in opposition to Hugo, without any of his pretentiousness, in fact on the very fringe of what is called
literature, a truly romantic drama established itself on
the "boulevard," the Broadway of Crime Alley. For
melodrama is the very essence of romantic drama in its
most justifiable aspect. We know its defects, its cult of
antithesis: its gross exaggerations make us laugh today,
with its characters as ridiculous as Triboulet and Marion
Delorme;[23] the bloodiest Elizabethan drama grows pale
beside its heaps of corpses. But at least it is honest, it
does not paint over its lies, it flatters public taste honestly
and with facts. Everything for action: closely knit, skillfully resolved, obvious to the most illiterate, it hurls its
actors around, shakes its stage wildly with thunder and
lightning. It injects into drama the dynamism Molière
achieved in farce and comedy, and in the end gives
semblance of reality to its shadows. It acts immediately
on the spectators. A true creator could have made valu-
able use of it, given it a human consecration.

Its great weakness was its self-sufficiency; it displaced
the center of drama, inalienably in the author, trans-

ferring it to the actor. Romantic melodrama came to mean its star actors, Frédéric Lemaître and Sarah Bernhardt,[24] rather than the almost forgotten writers of their scripts, Auguste Maquet and Sardou:[25] the tool became master of the craftsman. At first this genre had a healthy popularity, but it grew progressively corrupt as it gambled more and more on the dazzling talent of its actors and on vulgarized emotions, the emotions of cheap little dressmakers and fops of the *faubourg*. We have the skillful melodramas of Dumas *père,* and that is all: the expected master never came. But we must note one point: exterior action had been rehabilitated, it had regained the right to co-operate with the interior action, as in *Othello* and *King Lear*. So did Shakespeare's methods reach France.

During this time, comedy properly so called, asleep since Beaumarchais, woke up for the fifty-year reign of vaudeville under Eugène Scribe[26] and his rivals. Elaborate in intrigue, ingenious in the manipulation of a plot without human interest, tainted with maudlin sentimentality, its only value was the skill of the man who pulled the strings. Between vaudeville and melodrama, was there any room for a creative writer?

Indeed there was, but only by forsaking poetry, the very soul of the theatre since the days of Aeschylus. I shall explain later what I mean by poetry of the theatre. Bourgeois drama had destroyed it. Yet there was an exception, and I must pay him his due.

A man appeared, a young man, the most human of the great romantic poets, the least overburdened with aesthetic and humanitarian theories, the most genuinely French. He was Alfred de Musset.

He had all the qualifications to become a playwright, just the playwright we needed. He spoke a simple, limpid language, using the romantic jargon only as a dandyism and rather as a joke, with tongue in cheek. He knew men and loved them. His egocentrism? Only an attitude, reserved for his verse. In his blood ran the sweetest French tradition, equally Christian, gallant, and chivalrous. He loved the spontaneity of a Marivaux. Although he dabbled somewhat in the German romantics, he was never wholly taken in by them. His great admiration was for Shakespeare whom he understood and loved, not as a theory but as a friend. He was too sharp not to distinguish the purely British elements in Shakespeare from the universally human, the sixteenth-century crudities from all that was still acceptable in nineteenth-century France. He lightened, he filtered, he polished where it was needed; he handled the plays with subtlety and vitality, unlike the purely negative approach of the eighteenth-century Ducis. Thanks to his classical formation and natural affinity for the new, he held to the intersection point of traditions, the medieval tradition, returning to us at last through foreign lands, and the seventeenth-century tradition which he did not have the heart to reject. That was Musset's way of writing for the theatre. How was he appreciated?

After some first attempts in verse that were dramatic poems rather than true dramas (and in my opinion, unspeakable), he wrote one after another in prose at least ten plays in three years (1833-1835): *Barberine, Fantasio, The Follies of Marianne, No Trifling with Love, Chandler, Lorenzaccio,* and so on. They came crowding after one another in a creative outpouring.

Yet his first play was not to come before the footlights until 1847, and even then it was not one of those just named. In order to get on the stage, the poor author had to restrain his ambition and compose a parlor comedy for three characters—a little masterpiece at that—*Caprice*. Then all in one year (1848) it was decided to produce what I may call his Proverbs: *Chandler, A Door Must Be Either Open or Shut, Never Take an Oath*. These plays, which were not his best, had waited only three years. The other plays were left on the bookshelves until after his death they were finally discovered.

Was his art too closed? No, he is at every man's level. Too fragile? Perhaps. But where and how could he have gotten strength? He did not know the open air that challenges the mind, the free exchange that feeds and toughens it. Was he too free with established conventions—for example, the division of acts? I grant that. But if he had once seen his plays acted, if he had had experience with the tools his work required, the young playwright could have learned to make better use of them, to adapt his unbridled fantasy to the ways of the theatre. We do not know if his art would have lost or gained. Freedom from constraint might have allowed him to divine new possibilities for the stage; or he might only have followed the crowd and pandered to its passions with more intrigue, and less poetry. His art might have withered. But I am personally convinced that he would have overcome the obstacles, and little by little imposed his own law. His wellsprings would never have dried up: that vitality, that intuition of the human heart, that living lyricism which, in a lesser degree, he shared with Shakespeare. On the contrary the stage would have developed these very qualities. But for lack of proper tools, he remained a closet dramatist, conceiving his works only as unrealizable dreams. Why should he bother about the material means of embodying them? He wrote comedy "in his armchair," and, wearied of creating in a void, lost his fiery *élan*. When at last he saw his plays produced, they were not his best: his destiny was only half-fulfilled.

He had genius, but not good luck. His works, such as they are, testify to a marvelous gift, unique in his century. They blaze a new trail which a truly French dramatic art may follow up some day; an art that freely mingles comic and tragic, slipping easily from one level to the other, avoiding the too facile antithesis. Sorrow melts into joy, smiles into tears, life is many-sided, yet always of the same stuff; a poetic miracle unifies without falsifying. His people live, and know they live, but do not impale life on the blade of wit and word. A French Shakespeare brushed with Watteau's wings! For the first time in France, plot appears as a tale, airy and airborne, where nothing is essential but everything has its place. Intrigue relaxes tensions in a supple and capricious chain of events; secondary characters no longer exist only to provide cues, but in their own right, without distracting from the principals, plot develops in successive scenes moving through time and space, tracing a free curve, vibrant and winged.

Because Musset's plays were not for the stage, perhaps he may have abused his freedom. But we need only put these plays on the stage to test this. And at least he opposed the final degeneration of the Racine technique that substituted intrigue for plot in vaudeville and melodrama, with a new form, less abstract, less intellectual, full of unexpected resources, and with plenty of room for the free play of life and poetry.

II

But he was only a moment's intermission, a lone poet against the all-pervading realism. He had no followers except, at one period, Banville. Poetry was represented in the last years of the century only—and to my mind, unhappily—by a kind of romanticist tragedy called "play in verse," pseudo drama, with a few honest mediocre exceptions.

The poetic Musset wrote in prose yet his plays are poetic. Need I say more on that point? Until the day of the bourgeois theatre all playwrights had been poets not because they wrote in verse—look at Molière—but because they transposed reality to a new level of order, harmony, simplicity, by rhythmic beauty, plastic beauty, and freedom that exalted it to new nobility, new value. We see this in tragedy and comedy, Greek and medieval, in Shakespeare, Calderón, and in our own classics. To touch the audience, they expatriate it; by a deliberate withdrawal in time or space they set before it in the spirit of their own time particular exemplars of the great generality of mankind. The stage is a mirror in which reality sees itself not in its fleeting appearance, but in its abiding, eternal depths. Neither photography nor distortion, but rather transfiguration, if I may dare say this, the absolute opposite of naturalism, yet without violence to the natural, for nature is not changed but ordered. This necessary transposition—recall the first scene of *The Doctor in Spite of Himself*—affects the words, the gestures, the movements, the groupings, even the color pattern, composing a moving fresco that exactly mirrors the total action called for by the written text, written in fact in the very text itself. Such was and such is the theatre; such it has been in all times, under all skies, and today such should be what I call the poetry of theatre. Without it the theatre will not be itself. Musset understood that.

But the theatre turned its back on him. For next there came along the "modern play," half drama, half comedy, impossible to name exactly.

It is the heir, I repeat, of the still-born efforts of Diderot—who has ever read his *Père Prodigue*?—and of the melancholy comedy of Nivelle de La Chaussée. It exiled fiction, legend, and history, creative fantasy and tradition. The best it has to show us is the man in the street as we see him every day, his dress and speech and mannerisms wholly unmodified.

At least that is the purpose. It was not achieved at one blow, but for a whole century the movement has been in that direction.

Not that it is bad to keep in contact with reality. No playwright dares not do so. There is no interdict against observation of customs, ways, and character. What about Molière? But to paint is not to copy, and to cut close to the measure of actual life is the task of the novel, rather than of the stage. The fact is that the nineteenth-century bourgeois playwright took over the novelist's job and moved the novel into the theatre. Let us see what he made of it. If we must draw up a balance sheet, I could cite some plays of Émile Augier,[27] one of the chief plays of Becque[28]—not *Woman of Paris*, so superficial and dated, but *The Vultures*—almost all Ibsen's theatre, and a few other works of interest but of less value. These were exceptionally successful products of an art that does not and cannot transfigure. Tragedy by its very nature transfigures: it has the mask, the buskin, style; in it all things grow and expand. Comedy obeys the same law: it emphasizes and exaggerates, it swings daily language and natural behavior into its own rhythm. The same is true of farce and of those elements of farce, comedy, and tragedy that constitute Shakespearean drama. So too the Miracle play and the Mystery play. But there is nothing like this in the bourgeois play. It renounces "style" in the full sense of the word. To it, style is lying, deceitful, an insult to reality; we must accept the formless, honor and deify it as the only means of expression.

The two masters of this genre are Augier and Dumas *fils*.

Émile Augier established a few three-dimensional characters for he had a direct grasp of the real, though his grasp was still timid, weak, hampered by convention. He wrote in another age, yet he has influenced our times more than anyone else. I know some recent, solid, very creditable plays that are simply Augier rejuvenated. In fact, he laid the foundation for modern aesthetics, and only an ingrate would deny it. A real scoundrel, however, usurps his place: none other than Dumas *fils*. Augier was content with painting; Dumas had to preach. He introduced ideology into the bourgeois frame of reference, and pleaded his cases with legalistic casuistry. In all his plays the protagonist is the character least involved; it is the debater—Dumas himself—who always has a word to put in about marriage and divorce, adultery, and illegitimate children. He invented the "thesis play" with its innumerable offspring that are not always happy to acknowledge his paternity. It is strange that he still lives only in his first hit, *Camille* (*Lady with the Camelias*), that bourgeois flower of romanticism.

But now we have come to the threshold of our own period. Before crossing it, let us ask what has happened to the public.

This period corresponds roughly to the time between the wars of 1870 and 1914. It has formed us, we are its heirs. The public it has bequeathed us is not the public it received, yet a public that has evolved in a continuous line coming straight down to us through all the new ideologies, new institutions, and political fantasies. Whether this meant progress or retrogression, the fact is that what was true of the public in 1875 was still true in 1900 and until the eve of the First World War, and remained true even at its end. The nation had not broken down—the work of twenty centuries is not swept away in a hundred years—but society had broken up. There is in fact no real society today, no communal and provincial life such as created a certain cultural unity founded on religion in the Middle Ages, in spite of conflict and war; no national life like that of the seventeenth century centralized in Paris and the court, radiating out to the most distant provinces. There is nothing now to maintain a common idea of man, his duties, his needs, and, still less, any common concept of art. In the past every man shared more or less intimately in the general culture. It would be difficult to define the general culture of our day. Individualism and internationalism have begotten an endless multiplicity in our ways of feeling and thinking.

Each picks according to his own taste from the avalanche of newspapers, magazines, books that flood the country daily, or rather each picks according to the taste that has been imposed on him, without his realizing it, by advertising, fashion, party spirit, and propaganda; the same holds true of entertainment. Mechanized civilization has increased the amount of leisure in man's life, and consequently the amount of pleasure. People want films not only weekly but daily, while radios blast out full force all day long. I cannot give statistics, but there is no doubt that in no age did any people, even the Romans in their decadence, have at their disposal so many stages, loudspeakers, entertainers. It is abnormal; it is disastrous. But it is a fact.

Let us not forget that in the past the theatre was always something exceptional. With the Greeks it was performed as an act of worship only periodically on great festivals. In the Middle Ages, it was only at Christmas, Easter, and the feasts of patron saints. In the seventeenth century how many troupes of actors were there in Paris? Even the farces of Saint-Germain, Saint-Antoine, and the other theatres were not, I believe, given daily.[29] The corruption of public taste, especially in dramatic art, can be measured by our daily exploitation of not one but twenty theatres. There is multiplication and dispersion; there is no one public to rub elbows, to share in any community rejoicings—religious, national, or even local. The pleasure of playgoing has been cheapened, and so has the quality of the plays. We can enjoy them more often, so we ask less of them—greatly to the profit of their producers and agents. We are in the commercial, mass-production age of the theatre; financiers have taken it

over, and their aim is to give the spectator no more than
a minimum.

In this situation what happens to the author who still
believes dramatic art to be an art? To what unified and
sympathetic audience can he speak? There is no longer
a "public." There are a hundred publics. If he wants his
plays produced, he does not even have the choice between
a closed and a popular theatre. For a century the French
theatre has been neither the one nor the other, neither for
an elite nor for everyone. I hold that communion, the
very foundation of dramatic art, is equally necessary in
both cases: the closed theatre must have its aesthetic communication, the popular theatre its profound communion;
and these prerequisites can no longer be expected. We no
longer know with what we are dealing. Even in the case,
rare as it is, that we believe we have the elite or at least
one elite, how many in the group really agree on essentials? Do the intelligentsia form an elite? I doubt it,
if I may say this without giving offense. Still less does
the general public; it could no more agree on a play
than on morals or politics. And to think that this disintegrated world—the social world, the underworld,
the middle-class, upper and lower, the intellectuals, the
artists, and to some degree the laboring class, the white-
collar workers—all these together compose what we call
today "a full house." No two of them agree on the same
thing; no two of them applaud for the same reasons.

Since no communion can be either ensured or pre-
established, the author must create it entire. But the
problem is too complex; it puts into play too many
incalculable factors. Unless he takes a chance, unless he
gambles on it, he has nothing at all. So this difficult

collaboration tends fatally to force the man who is out for success to make concessions. The history of dramatic art in the last fifty years can be boiled down to the battle of a few resolute writers against an amorphous public, usually ending in defeat for the writers. The only alternative for the discouraged author is to make an unconditional surrender and flatter the public tastes that his predecessors have developed. In principle the public has no preferences, no tastes; it lets itself be captured by anyone who sets out to capture it, on condition that it be captured by what it wants. The producers of entertainment do not sin by omission here. As they cannot hope to touch the total public at the same time in the same way on the same sensitive point—aesthetic, moral, intellectual, or religious—they look lower, sure that they can always strike a sure blow at elemental sensuality. They pet it, they tickle it, they accustom it to expect this titillation. A discreet or cynical communing on the animal level, an appeal to the beast in man, such will soon be the shameful means of creating unanimity. Save for a few exceptions with vaguely literary or dramatic touches that demand a certain amount of talent, the bourgeois theatre has been perverted since the end of the nineteenth century into what we call boulevard theatre, a Broadway which for most men represents the true and only theatre. It is a special theatre for a special public, for it has polarized a certain group that sets the fashion for today's masses.

This degraded art had to have some aesthetic façade. Naturalism provided that.

But wait a moment. I am getting ahead of the facts. André Antoine had already founded the Théâtre Libre,[30] the earliest of the art theatres, closed theatres where the idea of a new drama would develop. Beneficial as his efforts were in some respects, nonetheless by speeding drama along the highway of "naturalism," he accelerated that decomposition whose dark portrait I have just drawn. Because of him, Porto-Riche, Bernstein, Bataille[31] have walked in the footsteps of Henry Becque without his power and his talent, and because of him so many authors today specialize in variations on adultery, that favorite theme, under the pretext of "truth." But first let us look at his good side.

III

When Antoine appeared, there is no doubt that the instrument needed repair. There had been too much harping on certain conventions, not wholly bad, but offensive both to liberty and reason. The dogma of the "well-constructed play" was still sacrosanct. This "well-constructed play" of Racine had little by little become that of Scribe, then that of Victorien Sardou. Every writer worshipped this sacred mechanism, whose wheels, since the death of Émile Augier, were turning in the void. Without substance, how could drama be alive and natural?

André Antoine tried to reacclimatize the theatre to life and nature, though perhaps he misunderstood them. At first he certainly went too far. I mentioned above the concept of the stage as a room with one wall missing, where men of today, just like you and me, live their dull little lives, indifferent to the audience that overhears and spies on them. That was his idea. He sought to replace the romantic actor playing to the audience with the realistic actor playing for himself alone. Both excesses are to be condemned, but in my opinion, the first less than the second; for despite its exaggeration, it maintains an exchange, a communication, while the second abolishes it completely. Truth lies in the mean, and a middle term was later sought. The romantic actor destroyed the sense of reality, he was nothing but actor; the classical actor (who also displeased Antoine), adopted techniques to express the essential meaning of his part, following but exaggerating a wise tradition. Against both these schools Antoine's actor, i.e., Antoine himself, was right on two points: first, he must learn from man himself, he must turn his back on the audience to seem more human. Antoine's very faults and deficiencies were those of the self-taught man who, amazed at his own discoveries, exaggerates their value. Secondly, he rescued something very precious by restoring the validity of gesture and speech. This is crucial, even if he did not give the stage a new and a living aesthetic; for it respects the person of man himself, his very being, and without that respect, there is no drama.

Exterior realism as a technique is always in danger of minutiae, unsuitable to the theatre and distracting it from its own primary aim of presenting local color in all its horror. But it could lead the dramatist to a more human approach to his art, an approach long abandoned by psychological realism. His concern for man's exterior truth could and did lead to the interior truth. In fact that is exactly the significance of Antoine, not to mention the many authors whom he inspired or discovered. At that time, that is, between 1880 and 1890, both author and actor had great need of being recalled to the realities of

life. He should have the credit for this. It is not his fault
if the movement first bogged down in the lowest naturalism and then was vulgarized on the boulevards instead
of being purified and deepened through the work of true
dramatists.

There was only one such, the author of *The Vultures*,[32]
but he was too often barren, too full of self-doubt, and
because of his very gifts not well received. He had something that Antoine and his friends necessarily lacked—
the sense of order, concision, style. Because of this his
work has endured. On another level, there was the great
and pure vision of the noble François de Curel; I will
return to him later.[33] The rest of them wrote good plays
without a spark of genius, already forgotten.

Antoine was worth more than his own theories. All
novelty was a temptation to him. Let us not forget that
his production of *The Wild Duck* first made Ibsen
known—so too he produced *Boubouroche*, that supreme
achievement of classic realism by Courteline, in which
the spirit of Molière lived again. And in regard to stag-
ing, let us not forget what he did for Shakespeare in the
boulevard theatre of Strasbourg and at the Odéon. These
productions mark a date in dramatic history as precursors
to the work of Firmin Gémier.[34] But most important
was the technical and moral influence of his initial effort.
In order to change the theatre, he decided first of all to
change the actor. The thorough but often mechanical
training of the Conservatory had rigidly codified the
acting techniques at our disposal. It was necessary to
revitalize them, at the risk of creating a more vulgar
pattern. Beneath the vulgar lies the natural, and vul-
garity's very failures only expose it; that is what hap-

pened. Naturalness is not everything, I must repeat, but
it is a good starting point, without which the artifice of
dramatic convention, essential in art, cannot exist. I will
even say that although the "slice of life," that old war
horse of naturalism, is not theatre—yet the theatre can
and must cut its own slice. To sum up the reform: there
was some recovery of the natural, some further loss of
style, or rather a final loss of style. By what door could
style re-enter, style that springs from poetry? We shall
discuss that in my last chapter.

4: FROM THE VIEUX-COLOMBIER
TO THE *Plays for the Faithful*

WE ARE coming to the end of this discussion. I do not pretend to offer you a comprehensive analysis of the whole French theatre either in the distant or the more recent past. You have no right to complain about the former—how could I ever treat it adequately? The seventeenth-century theatre obviously did not consist of Corneille, Racine, and Molière alone; their contemporaries may not even have realized how great they were. A hundred other comedies surround, support, explain Molière's comedy; a hundred other tragedies do the same for Racine and Corneille. But in any age its writers all work within the framework of an accepted norm of aesthetics and custom-imposed morality that is the same for all. Their combined efforts in one direction within this uniform climate create a "period" of drama—or a period of poetry or painting or music, and make a masterpiece possible. For only periods that possess such a unified culture are great and they alone produce masterpieces; no masterpiece is an isolated phenomenon. To speak of the masterpiece, then, is to imply all the others; that is all that I can do here.

It is not so easy to circumscribe the immediate past, the nineteenth and early twentieth centuries. They are too close; it is hard to see their big lines; the process of selection is only beginning. This task is even more difficult because in our grandparents' day there was an enormous increase in theatres and audiences, and therefore a reckless spawning of playwrights, plays, types of plays. Yet this has its commendable side. Never perhaps in any other age, even the most fruitful, has so much talent been spent on dramatic art, in fact, on all the arts. No, there is no lack of works, but *work* is lacking, or rather that common bond between works, incomplete, inferior, unsuccessful works though they be, the bond that alone creates a space for a true *work* to be born, and, once born, to live and to endure.

Nevertheless, let us beware of exaggeration. How do we know that posterity will not see the romantic period in terms of Musset's fantasies, two or three bourgeois comedies of Augier and the *Faiseur* of Balzac, tied together by Labiche's vaudeville; or the naturalistic period as Becque's *Vultures* with a few farces by Courteline and Feydeau? How do we know that the textbooks will not thus create a venerable and fictitious unity from these plays of this confused era? It is an old trick.

But yesterday's past, still close enough to touch—how sum that up, how characterize it without blatant injustice? Criticism must make the attempt—and often fool itself in the process. Read Sainte-Beuve and see how often he was wrong about contemporaries, infallible as he was when looking back over a long stretch of time. But criticism must accept this obligation with all its dangers in order to help its own day to see clearly, to free itself from confusion, to encourage production in the most promising direction. The duty of the producer, whether he writes plays or stages them, is no less imperious. To avoid any strong stand, any narrow and even violent partisanship, to try to be fair toward all contemporaries, is to elect sterility. I warned you at the beginning that I would speak not as a critic but as a writer, a producer, and even a businessman. My ideas are not only incomplete but deliberately partial.

I

I have summarized briefly the situation as it was a few years before World War I. The heresy of "naturalism" had already produced its effect: the Théâtre Libre was everywhere. Its emphasis on exterior likeness to truth led to consideration of inner truth. But the subject matter was very restricted. Our dramatic psychologists— or those who so styled themselves—exploited adultery exclusively, though it is really not so popular as all that, nor is it our main occupation; in consequence the triangle was always with us. Some naturalness was regained but all notion of style was lost. I have more to say about that.

Style, the poetry proper to the theatre (you know now what that means), had fled to pure poetry; and today's pure poetry is symbolist poetry, the most closed poetry any age has ever produced. Even more subjective than romantic poetry, it is conceived for the secret and egotistic delight of its writer. It hardly allows a few initiates entrance. Hence it creates most unfavorable dispositions for the invention and projection of characters distinct from the poet himself, and for any exchange of thought with an audience. Yet from these *cénacles* of symbolism emerged Maurice Maeterlinck, Paul Claudel, and also—our sorrow and our shame—Henri Bataille. I could cite other names—Émile Verhaeren,[35] Francis Vielé-Griffin,[36] or André Gide,[37]—they are all primarily poets, and only accidentally, occasionally, are they dramatists. Yet they have something to teach professional playwrights. For the first three named above, to whom I will add Maurice de Faramond and, on the borders of naturalism, Curel, represent the idealistic or poetic reaction. I omit Hervieu[38] and put Paul Bourget in a class by himself, for he is more novelist than dramatist; Rostand[39] adds nothing, save a final glamorization of Hugo's picaresque drama. Plays written only for reading, such as those of Villiers de l'Isle-Adam, Élémir Bourges, Péladan,[40] are obviously not our concern here.

The Théâtre de l'Oeuvre was founded by Lugné-Poë[41] and his gifted actress-wife, Suzanne Despres, in opposition to the Théâtre Libre. But it won no decisive victory on the field of symbolist poetry. It produced poems like *La Gardienne* of Henri de Régnier, and later Francis Jammes' *Un Jour,*[42] as unfit for the stage as any poem could be. They played a little of Maeterlinck, and later some of Claudel, but foreign authors were their chief line; I shall come back to this. Do you know the Oeuvre's chief title to the gratitude of theatre-lovers? The presentation of *Ubu Roi,* received as it was with a chorus of whistles, hisses, protests, and jeers—I was there myself. Alfred Jarry,[43] a university student engaged in the familiar enterprise of making fun of a professor, unwittingly had created a masterpiece, a boldly blocked, darkly concentrated assault, in the style of Shakespeare

and of Punch and Judy. It is an epic satire on the bourgeois, the avaricious and cruel bourgeois, exploiter of the
masses. Whatever meaning you give it, Jarry's *Ubu Roi*
is one hundred per cent theatre as we say today, pure,
synthetic theatre, stretching conventions to the point of
shock, creating realistic symbolism on the very margin
of reality. I salute Alfred Jarry, the precursor—who had
no followers.

Maeterlinck dealt with mood and mystery, moving
with animated shadows. Unless I am mistaken, "at-
mosphere" theatre dates from him, that drama in which
environment overwhelms and disintegrates the characters
that breathe and move in it. They emerge from the unconscious, not made explicit in word as in classical
drama, nor implicit in action as in Shakespeare . . . and
in Jarry. The cloak of mystery from then on wrapped
itself around drama. Not that we should exclude mystery
and the unconscious from the theatre, for there is room
for everything. But does not the exploitation of these two
elements belong to music more than to the spoken word?
In fact I have already shown, in a chapter of *Nos Directions*,[44] how the Maeterlinck formula of symbolist drama
finds literary artifices inadequate, mere repetitions, stam-
merings; it can be realized fully only in musical form
as when *Pelléas* is transfigured by the genius of Claude
Debussy. A spoken dramatic art, the only one with which
we are here concerned, cannot remain so near the fron-
tiers of music without being tempted to enter. That is its
destiny, perhaps its duty. For if it does not cross the line,
it turns into a false and fictitious hybrid, like the preten-
tious theatre of that pseudo poet, Henri Bataille. Let us
now dispose of him.

A man like Bataille is basically indistinguishable from the boulevard playwright. He emerged from the Théâtre de l'Oeuvre, but quickly became acclimatized to the milieu where he made his career. The subjects he treats, the creatures he paints would have been at home with Henry Bernstein. I must admit, however, that I infinitely prefer Bernstein. He is honest, he gives himself for what he is, he has legitimatized a realistic sketchy and brutal melodrama, with great audience appeal. He handles gross human material, but with power and decision. He is direct and, believe it or not, traditional, with nothing oblique in his approach. His language is banal but bare, without the least literary pretentiousness. But Henri Bataille demands first rank among his boulevard peers, posing as poet, artist. Read his prefaces to see the scope of his ambition. He wants his theatre to create not the portraits of a few men, but of all mankind; to present not some aspects of life, but all Life, yes Life with a capital L—drama and poetry, the conscious and the unconscious, all concrete reality, all mystery, in a word, the entire universe. You may say that this is a Catholic concept; perhaps so—but without law, without dogma, i.e., without order.

His ambitions are not all Utopian. He insists on the value of silence, of music:

"Play two measures on the piano; no one can ever know how much love I put in these two measures . . . this melody is you."

Again he writes: "The pure exclamation is far more significant than the sentence. What can replace the pathos of a gesture, of a silence, of an inarticulate sound?"

He leaves it to the spectator to guess what is behind the cry, the silence, the two or three notes; and it is the job of the set-designer, the electrician, the violin soloist, the accordion-player, the street singer in the courtyard or the piano upstairs to express what he does not say and is quite incapable of saying. That is his idea of poetry. Note that none of these means would discredit a playwright provided he used them honestly and not just to get out of the difficulty of thinking and expressing his thought with precision, of writing and selecting his words with care. "The school of silence" has been founded. Make room for the set-designer, who supplies script and business! The kingly word has been put in its place as a mere accessory; it no longer patterns, orders, and builds the play. Bataille's aesthetic doctrine is the enemy of all design, and therefore of all great art. Drama has evaporated.

Bataille's plays are superabundant proof of how such contempt for the word leads to abuse of language, falsified emotion, falsified poetry, the worst kind of "literature." His characters swim in a kind of lyric sauce which quickly dissolves what meager reality they had. Was Bataille the precursor of Wagner's synthetic theatre, that supposed imitation of the Greeks? He believed he was. But what he called synthesis was mixture, mush, that could only end in zero.

His theories led directly to the Théâtre Libre with its exact reproduction of the appearances of reality. They forgot that the word is a germinating seed. The stronger, the stricter, the more charged with meaning and life it is, the more it ought to be written before it is spoken: it bears on the moment and admits no delay. They forgot that the theatre's truth lies in one thing: that the part possess the actor's soul. All the rest is false façade, especially the sets. Forest, city, and sea will never be anything but painted canvas. The theatre demands *a different concept of space,* not enclosed within four walls, *a different concept of time,* not measured by our watches, *a language of signs.* Then we can evoke plains and sea, mountain and city, even heaven and hell, as did the medieval mysteries, but always *without picturing them.* Or else let us shut ourselves up forever in a bourgeois parlor, a nightclub, an attic, minutely designed, lighted, furnished. If our taste is good, we shall create pleasant genre pictures—which add nothing to the play and will never express its meaning.

I would have liked to say more about the dramatic work of Paul Claudel.[45] The idealistic or rather the spiritual reaction against naturalism, healthier than in Bataille, stronger than in Maeterlinck, reached in him its fulfillment. A true playwright and a great playwright, he is first of all a writer—a great writer. He does not make too much use of silence or scenery or projections to say what he has not said or what he "says without saying it." Perhaps in fact he says too much. In him we see an acute conflict between practical playwright and poet— each in turn using and abusing the other. Perhaps his lyric temperament is too strong for him; in any case it has been encouraged to excess by the closed milieu in which he has worked, by the masters he has chosen, by the solitude in which he has lived. Nonetheless his drama is rich and violent. His overflowing lyricism is inevitably hampered by the present condition of the theatre; hence he seems to have resigned himself to the fact that drama as he conceives it is unattainable today. In consequence he has given free rein to words and images; he works the whole play out in the script, even the sets, the lights, the musical accompaniment, the sound effects. This is well-meant, but goes too far. When his language grows bare, however, when his characters clash in a rapid, concise, profound exchange seemingly in spite of him, by some inner necessity of the climactic action, as in some scenes of *The Exchange* and the first plays, this is indeed the return of *style* to stage dialogue.

We can follow his growth as a playwright from *The City* to *The Hostage*: little by little, without renouncing his lyric gift, he subordinates it to the exigencies of dramatic art; little by little he learns his way around the stage, makes himself at home there, and finally begins to assert his power over it, giving it new dimensions. The second act of *The Hostage* and the *Tidings Brought to Mary,* though still richly poetic, are, in my opinion, the two peaks of his dramatic achievement; no one in our day has written anything that surpasses or even equals them in terms of theatre.

Claudel's concept of drama is truly Catholic, firmly based and patterned on dogma and faith. Man has his place, God has his place, so too the whole universe and the clash and conflict of human souls under the hand of God. Such is the substance of a work centered on the divine, growing from within like an enormous oak, heavy with leaves and living sap that flows out to the smallest twig. There is nothing arbitrary, nothing for pure ornamentation in spite of the luxuriance; and in this it is classical.

His power as a dramatist had long been questioned. But the first performance of the *Tidings*, poor as it was, came as a happy surprise: on the stage his tense involved style proved far more comprehensible than on the printed page —a dazzling demonstration and proof that his is the true dramatic word.

Yet the struggle still goes on. Claudel's art, made for immense space, is stifled in the "little" theatre. He lacks the means of practicing his art; long exile has separated him from the stage and the audience in which his drama could take flesh. He has been resigned to this too long even to speak of it, save to intimate friends. It is both his fault and ours. Had there been a larger elite, less divided in itself, more in communication with the masses, the public would have accepted him unanimously; and, learning the laws of communication by actual experience, he would have had more success in controlling his poetry and expanding his thought.

Claudel will remain Claudel, however fashions may change, and he has not yet reached the end of his career. He is of the line of Aeschylus, Shakespeare, Calderón; what do his defects matter against that magnificent ancestry? Because he is more European than French, more universal than European, he honors France the more.

Yet it would seem that Claudelianism will not survive long on our stage. His art is so peculiar to its author that, while we can learn from him lessons of nobility, plenitude, concentration, we cannot imitate him. It would be insane to try. Like all geniuses too great for their own times, Claudel stands alone. He has had great influence in French lyric poetry—not always for the best; his influence on the stage is either very slight, or very far in the future. We must be content to work humbly in his shadow.

II

To speak of the symbolist movement in drama is to recall the Scandinavian writers, Björnson, Strindberg, and above all Ibsen. The "pure aesthete" snobs have made a cult of Ibsen, now as an integral symbolist and again as a propagandist, and all the while he is quite simply a good bourgeois realist who uses symbols and is not afraid of ideas. He has been misinterpreted on the stage too, and solemnly laid to rest to the singing of psalms. He is so alive, so natural; yet he has been made the essence of boredom, morose sermonizing and affectation. In fact he has been betrayed and perverted into a harmful influence.

Did this influence somehow cause the half-failure of a now forgotten playwright, Maurice de Faramond, who vanished before he achieved his full measure? I am afraid so. Faramond invented a kind of synthetic realism, a parody of symbolism, best seen in his *Noblesse de la Terre*. Only in the powerful writings of François de Curel, *Le Repas du Lion*, *La Nouvelle Idole*, does ideological drama, in the Dumas-*fils* tradition of the thesis play, succeed in overcoming its own antidramatic elements. Curel was a great artist, not to be confused with the mediocre naturalists around him. It would take too long to explain here why, save in satiric comedy, the stage cannot be a battlefield for ideas, unless the ideas have taken human flesh and bone and face. Maurice de Faramond and François de Curel did achieve that miracle several times, but their followers failed them and their work needs to be begun anew.

It seems that there are too many possibilities open before us, too many different roads, all equally attractive.

One way alone, one good way, would be more fruitful. Dramatic art is unsure of itself, condemned to a complexity or 'rather an anarchy of dispersed effort. Yet in spite of all this, just before the first World War and just after Antoine, it came to a stalemate: novelty of form went dead. I do not include in this death the charming and absolutely trivial Parisian entertainment of the Théâtre des Variétés—cocktails by Flers and Caillavet, mixed with Meilhac and Halévy; nor the often-pleasant irony of Capus and Donnay[46] whose elegance and poetic sensitivity are closer to dramatic truth than the false psychology of Porto-Riche, the so-called Jewish Racine. Bernstein and Bataille still ruled the tragic stage. In this *impasse,* technical invention alone could, and finally did, renew dramatic art. Certain curious experiments in expansion and liberation of set design were made in Shakespearean production by Antoine and Gémier in France, Gordon Craig in England, Appia in Italy,[47] Max Reinhardt in Germany, as well as in the decorative innovations of Jacques Rouché in the Théâtre des Arts, the Ballet Russe of Serge Diaghilev and Stanislavski's fusion of style with realistic precision.[48] Some twenty years earlier, it is true, the new painters—Vuillard, Bonnard, Seruzier, Maurice Denis—had designed sets for Lugné-Poë's undramatic symbolist poetry at the Oeuvre. But the essential is acting, not the set; the set is for the acting, in function of the acting, and fantastic drapes serve it no better necessarily than photographic comic-opera backdrops. The chief goal of all these efforts was a more diversified, freer, three-dimensional stage to allow Shakespearean drama a continuity of fluid movement in time and space. Perhaps this might have inspired new playwrights to bold innovation, had it not been dropped too soon. But applied only to sacrosanct masterpieces, it ended up in a barren virtuosity hitherto the exclusive prerogative of the actor. Antoine's great service was to make the actor again a part and not the whole show, by reviving the traditional company or acting troupe.

This is where Copeau comes in. He needs no introduction, for you all know him, and no defense, for we are all his friends, fans, and disciples. In 1913 this theatre, this Vieux-Colombier where we are now holding these discussions, was only an entertainment hall—the Saint-Germain Athenaeum, where amateurs disported themselves. Today we see what he has made of it. He built from nothing, began in genuine poverty. That is exactly what the theatre needs today; it has gotten too expensive, too extravagant, too showy. His work is indisputably superior to all that went before or has followed him and his superiority is of the spirit. Jacques Copeau knew what he wanted, he weighed the risk, adapted the tools at hand. He was convinced of one thing: the primacy of the actor—the actor who is the very warp and woof of the play, the living presence of the author, giving substance and life to his design. Everything is done by the actor and for the actor; all the rest is superfluous. On the bare stage, against a gray curtain, the action itself had to carry all the symbolism, all the suggestion, all the significance. Later, after 1918, he devised a more elaborate and adjustable set where the actors could move on many levels of proscenium, platforms, balconies. The principle that he had laid down from the beginning was a movement and value arrangement of the human elements of the play in rhythmic and plastic order to express the essence of the action in the most legible, accurate, and emphatic pattern. "A platform, two sticks and two passions," Calderón said, I believe—that is an essential and adequate definition of Copeau's scenic art.

You either like such total nakedness or you don't. You may prefer the painted canvas and wooden planks of the Italian stage or a neutral cyclorama with solid concrete floor. That matters little. It is either one fiction or another; dramatic art is always a make-believe. What is the best make-believe, or, rather, the most suggestive, the most significant symbol? That is the whole question. In the actor's presence all these conventions suddenly take on life. He is a man like other men, a man who might have been a beggar or a king; he comes on the stage in rags or golden robes, believing that he is a king or a beggar—if he really believes it, he will be it. Complete identity is possible between the character as conceived by the author and as realized by the actor, on condition that the actor enters deeply into his part, exteriorly and interiorly, i.e., both by his technical skill and by his humanity. Then, and only then, will he serve the play honestly, collaborate to bring the whole work to life. I need not speak of the training, the integrity, and the dedication that this demands of the actor. Such was the origin of the Company and the School of the Vieux-Colombier.

The stage and the actor thus regained their original meaning, their essential and primordial function: no more and no less than to serve the author's idea, to make it legible, intelligible, in form and rhythm, convention and reality, keeping what is natural without the banality or corruption of the naturalistic school, preserving style without the pomposity and absurdity of the Conservatory fossil; to live in acting and act in living; all that for the actors. Copeau's stage gives them a practicable area with breadth and depth and height in which to move, thanks to the varied stage levels on which they can successively group and separate, filling the entire stage with arabesques or mass patterns emphasized by the costume color scheme—all in order to project the inner meaning of the play. Significant handling of set, lighting, and incidental music illuminate and support the word and movement.

Such are the elements of Jacques Copeau's reform of stage design. He did not invent, but brought tradition back to life for our day. All the attempts that have followed, except perhaps those of Georges Pitoëff and Gaston Baty, owe everything to him. Charles Dullin and Louis Jouvet learned their craft on this stage; the Vieux-Colombier is father of us all.

What a tool for a playwright! It can serve as well for Musset as for Molière, for Marivaux as for Shakespeare. The incrustations are at last scraped off their great plays, and they come alive before us in their proper genius. It has served André Gide (*Saül*), Jean Schlumberger (*La Morte de Sparte*), Jules Romains (*Cromedeyre le Vieil*), Roger Martin du Gard (*Le Testament du Père Leleu*), Georges Duhamel (*L'Oeuvre des Athlètes*), and Mazaud, Porché, René Benjamin. I patterned *The Beggar under the Stairs* in terms of the methods learned here, for it was here that I completed my dramatic education. This art is worlds away from the degraded realism of the modern French stage; it is free and harmonized, truthful and stylized, solid and flexible, a bridge between Musset, Shakespeare, and Molière. Copeau's very insistence on those great plays opened a new door to us and to young writers, a door to the tradition of our most distant past, the tradition whose course these talks have tried to map out. Today the Atelier is presenting Alexandre Arnoux's *Hugh of Bordeaux,* a powerful and exquisite play that shows what is possible by a return to dramatic truth, at the point where bourgeois realism broke away.

III

But do not try to fence in the field now open to the many young playwrights, new since 1918. I cannot read their future in the stars, but it does not take a horoscope to see that the stage's renewed technique is a powerful attraction to the new writers.

Note that I say "writers." Do not forget the aberration of the past—that fatal separation of literature from drama: eliminating writers from the stage, and dramatists from literature. Even if to be a good writer does not necessarily make you a playwright, to be a good playwright you must be a good writer too. But the divorce has now ended; the hermetically sealed *"cénacles"* of subjectivism are no longer in style; everywhere we feel the need for communion, for getting out of the self, for confronting the other, communicating with the other. Such exchange is not easy of attainment in the deepening moral and intellectual anarchy. But the desire for it is there, in every group, even the most *avant-garde,* all claiming some kind of order—Marxist, republican, monarchist, all demanding a society. I do not assert that the theatre can re-create society, but it can help in the work of re-creation. No longer in Olympian isolation, literary men now realize they will not lose prestige if they entertain the spectator.

Comedy is coming to life again with Benjamin, Romains, Marcel Achard; in fact, the main tendency is toward comedy and farce, so congenial to neo-Shakespearean drama. Literature actually dares laugh and make others laugh; it has returned to sanity! [49]

But will the public laugh? Is there, indeed, any public to laugh the same laugh—except the conditioned low vaudeville laugh? When men are without a true society, a true center, they do not laugh or weep at the same things. A new public, however, can be created. That is what we are working for at the Vieux-Colombier, the Atelier, the Comédie des Champs-Elysées, the Chimère, the Petite Scène, even at the Comédie-Française where simpler and organic production is gaining ground.[50] This new public is recruited in part from among those not unfamiliar with theatre—writers, artists, men of taste— but in part only, for they would not be enough to fill even the tiniest theatre every night. If they were the only audience—we would have another closed theatre for a new elite. Is that what we want? I hope not. Look at Marivaux: see in him how anemic that kind of theatre is, how disintegrated, how out of touch with reality. It cannot synthesize or keep the balance between the exotic and the trite; its subjectivism excludes man himself. Therefore we need a more varied and less intellectual public to join the elite in the theatres of tomorrow. The old problem then comes up again: if an author refuses to resort either to sophistication or to suburban sentimentality—*on what basis will he be understood?*

Perhaps the basis of understanding is man himself? In theory, yes, a writer's power to contact an audience is in proportion to the humanity of his art. In theory, men ought to agree on certain general sentiments—but in fact, they agree on them less and less. Any agreement is only fortuitous, some issue polarizes and fuses for a moment a certain category of the audience: something in the air, a political allusion, a scandal. . . . We must face it, but the risk is great, for such polarization is incalculable. A writer with something real to produce needs a steady normal career in the theatre, like that of Shakespeare or Molière, whose plays were guaranteed immediate production. The modern stage will never produce what it should until there is a public again, until society is reborn.

However, I know one remedy for immediate relief, although it is closed to most playwrights, i.e., religion. It demands faith, piety, and the firm will to build on them. I would not even mention this if I were the only one concerned. But there are still many Catholics in France— and an enduring Catholic mentality. There are playwrights, too, who do not conceive of their art as completely separate from their faith. I have a proposal for them. I offer them quasi-ideal conditions of dramatic creation; I offer them theatre, actors, and a public. They need not sacrifice all contact with the secular theatre and its composite, incoherent audience. They can compete there like everyone else when they get a chance. But in the meantime let them speak to the "faithful" (*le peuple fidèle*), meet them on the common ground of the faith. If art is man's highest expression, what right have we to exclude from it the thoughts and feelings by which he raises himself to God? Who can forbid him to express them in the theatre? Was not the theatre itself born from religion? All my own effort and achievement has been based on this religious concept of theatre. However Utopian my dream or mistaken my effort, the principle is healthy, conforming entirely to Copeau's axiom, worth repeating again:

There will never be a new theatre until the day comes when the man in the audience murmurs in his heart and with his heart the same words spoken by the man on the stage.

Copeau here admits that long experience has taught him it is not enough for author and audience to share the same concept of art alone in order to achieve mutual understanding.

After an event that completely changed my life,[51] and made me one of the faithful again after many years, I began to dream of fusing my faith with my art. Or rather, this happened in spite of me. I came by chance upon a Christian subject for a play; it interested me, I did my best with it, not worrying about its production or reception. That was how I wrote that very lyric, very personal play, *The Three Miracles of Saint Cecilia*. At the end of the war, the Vieux-Colombier reopened; five years earlier it had produced my *L'Eau de Vie*. Now I wrote my second religious play for it, for it alone: *The Beggar under the Stairs*. In writing it, I took the same risk as for a secular play. *The Beggar* shocked some and touched others, but changed nothing for me. Then one day a great friend, Maurice Denis, asked me to work on a play for a parish production. He was angry and alarmed at the poor quality of the religious plays then being produced and thought that perhaps an artist might be able to raise the level, even a little. Why not? I tried, and did my very best, though I did not know the group for which I was writing, nor its usual repertory; I sought only to be simple, sincere, direct. That was the *Farce of the Hanged Man Unhanged,* based on a miracle from the Golden Legend. It first was played to an unsympathetic audience in a new legitimate theatre at Montmartre; but when produced in its true environment, it turned out to be a surprising hit. That determined my destiny. It opened my eyes to a truth no doubt long germinating in my mind, a truth on which I base all I have said here: that dramatic art can attain its purity and plenitude only when there is already in existence a conscious and willed agreement between author and audience, as Copeau was to say later. Yes, in my case, practice preceded theory; theory only confirmed and justified it. It was a tremendous discovery to find that the desperately needed communion between audience and stage already actually existed, at least for a Catholic, in that lowly and limited set-up, the parish theatre. A good lesson in humility.

The communion in such a theatre is based on matter, not on form, but this is the first and essential communion; given time, the second will follow. If the writer speaks clearly enough, it is impossible not to understand. The truth he speaks is true for everyone; all agree with him about what is true and false, evil and good. A parish audience is a very mixed gathering of children and women, day-laborers and white-collar workers, first-graders and intellectuals; opinions differ about everything else but not about the faith. All have the same concept of the world, of the natural and the supernatural, of man and his duties, of the soul and its destiny, of dogma, the commandments, of the reality of the Incarnation, of the Father and of the Spirit. I am a Christian, a Roman Catholic; their concept is mine. We face each other on the same level—and so too does the actor.

This same dream came at the end of his life to the translator of Gerhart Hauptmann's *The Weavers*.[52] He listed lovingly all the parishes of France, that litany dear to Péguy, dreaming of each with its own stage and group of actors. What a dream: a popular and Christian drama, a true drama, suddenly or by a slow struggle, wresting the stage away from those nameless mediocrities that have enslaved it for centuries. That would indeed be something new—and something great.

We would again have something of the privileged position of the medieval playwright. Immense crowds gathered in the streets to see the Mysteries, but in our parish audience too, would be a small but accurate image of total Christianity—all ages, all classes, all trades, all levels of culture, bound together in the unity of faith, *religio*.

It would be a powerful help to the faith, that goes without saying. But also it would benefit culture and benefit dramatic art itself, freeing it both from its little cliques of elite and from the degradations of pandering to the masses at their worst. We won't be one hundred percent successful: if we try to speak to everyone, no one will take in everything. Yet everyone will get something. The author's obligation is to give to each, from the most highly educated to the simplest folk, as much as each can take in. This is a serious challenge but not a new one. Sophocles had to face it, as well as Gréban. It is not peculiar to Christian drama; it is the problem of all drama, and one that can never be solved easily. But a Christian environment does make a solution possible.

Themes? There are plenty: there is an enormous unexploited treasure of gaiety, emotion, faith, and crudity too. The Middle Ages were too immature to use it; the classicists too uninterested; the romanticists too vague. The French Shakespeare able to mold this material into a national Christian drama never appeared. Today we have the chance to do it, a unique opportunity to cultivate a living slip from the old medieval tree of life.

Copeau's work is the exemplar for the production groups we must form. Amateurs may not have the skill or flexibility of the Vieux-Colombier actors, but the chief virtue of soul—and body—to renew or develop in the actor is sincerity, ingenuousness. The school or parish actor will find this in himself if we can help him look for it. We will get a different kind of emotion and action, lacking of course in virtuosity, but that does not matter; it will have its own charm, as I have found in working with very young people. It gives the playwright a wholly new register. The modern stage is moving toward simplicity, austerity; it will be easy to do something with almost nothing except a little taste, as we learned from the practices and principles of Jacques Copeau's reform.

Then there is the audience. But I have said enough about that. Save for a few hopeless cases, people will be delighted to get away from the banality of our usual entertainment. They will be enlarged, educated; they will enjoy their faith, and without realizing it, be led to a truer concept of art.

The presentation of evil may be somewhat restricted, chiefly in regard to sex, but the passion of love is not the only one worth describing. . . . Moreover, art flourishes under restraint: first comes adjustment, then even greater achievement.

Such are the facts. I am not talking of dreams. I have personally experimented with all this. What is still a dream—until the new order of things—is that a large group of serious playwrights should begin to write for school and parish theatre, subjecting themselves to the laws of the genre without compromising their art. This needs the organization of guilds to produce plays on great feasts for the whole parish, for all the faithful. But though our dreams have not yet been realized, the time will come soon. I do not want to advertise my personal achievements, but there is not a week without some new production in France, Belgium, Switzerland; I often take part in it, training the actors, improvising sets, observing the audience . . . doing my job. There are obstacles but not insurmountable ones. There are occasional catastrophes, but nine out of ten succeed. Some of these plays would act well on this very stage where I am addressing you now: for example, *Saint Cecilia,* or *The Wonderful Adventures of Giles,* first produced at the Collège de Saint-Aspais in Melun, or *Death on Horseback,* written for the parish of Saint-Roch, and repeated recently in Flanders on a small-town stage, and lastly *Saint Maurice,* given in the abbey of Saint-Maurice in the Valais and repeated with equal success in the parishes of Saint-Roch and of Notre Dame de Lorette.

All this proves that I have not wasted my time, that the idea has spread enormously in only three years. Others will take it up and do still better. In the meantime I do my job under conditions that the most favored playwright could envy. When I write something for an audience, I can try it out immediately on that very audience. Twelve of the fifteen plays written in the last five years have been produced, and the thirteenth will open on Sunday.[53]

I have no excuse for not producing good plays.

But that is enough about myself. Others are beginning to follow. There is Henri Brochet,[54] who writes charming morality plays. Some began before me, especially René Des Granges, whose *Saint Germain* will be given at Auxerre for the saint's feast. I myself have been asked to produce a *Mystery of Saint Bernard of Menthon*[55] to be staged near Annecy on the terrace of the tenth-century castle in which the saint was born. One step more and we will be putting up our platforms at the church doors.

The time may come—and it is not as far off as we think—when on all the great Church feasts an art will flower wholly in harmony with its environment. Three years ago, no one could have dreamed of that as even possible.

In other environments that do not share the ancient faith, a secular drama may also achieve a wide level of communication. Whatever that level may be, I hold that drama is absolutely dependent on the solid reality of a communion. For our craft has now all it needs to develop: it has writers, directors, actors; all it needs is an audience.

Appendix: Fifteen Years Later

I STILL hold today all that I said in 1923 in the four talks given in the Vieux-Colombier shortly before Jacques Copeau left that theatre. I do not take back one word, one principle, one prophecy.

Bourgeois realism has continued to go downgrade, and still dominates the professional stage.

The Paris theatre is represented by the amazing Sacha Guitry,[56] who too often wastes his talents. With other ambitions he might have become the Molière or the Beaumarchais of today's fashionable world. He had all the power and vitality needed, but succumbed to cheap success.

The most important phenomenon of the last fifteen years has been the triumph of Copeau's reform through the work of his disciples. As you know, he left the Vieux-Colombier and brought his school of acting to Pernand, a now famous little village in Burgundy. With the help of Mme. Suzanne Bing, he tried to rebuild his work from the ground up with very young boys and girls, unspoiled by Conservatory methods. He initiated them into pure acting and improvisation, techniques of the mask, speech, mime, and "style." The *Copiaux*, as he called them, went from town to town, from village to village, through the whole province and neighboring provinces, even to foreign countries, Switzerland and Belgium. But Paris never saw them and no one spoke of Copeau any more.

Nevertheless the *avant-garde* theatres that had sprung from him kept his teaching alive. The fiery enthusiasm of Dullin's group and the careful detail of Jouvet's direction drew larger audiences and expanded the elite. Hence today Dullin's Atelier, Jouvet's Athenée, and the similar groups of Pitoëff's Mathurins and Gaston Baty's Théâtre Montparnasse, draw audiences as large as and far more intelligent than those of the boulevard theatres.[57] Yet they have had to make concessions to the general public and its taste. Their writers had dreamed of restoring poetry to the theatre, but little by little were forced to turn to self-frustrating, semi-realistic, semi-Parisian techniques. Pitoëff and Dullin, the most intransigent of the four, had to fall back on the great works of the past: Molière, Shakespeare, Calderón, Balzac, Musset, and Chekhov, and only in this way succeeded in holding to the essentials.

Then for some mysterious reason Jacques Copeau abandoned his own company and his own school. His actors founded the Compagnie des Quinze in Paris, taking over the Vieux-Colombier again, but after three years and some brilliant moments of success, the group finally broke up. They however had given their master's doctrine its definitive form with the help of André Obey, the playwright,[58] who followed this doctrine in all its rigor. No one can forget the *Noah*, the *Rape of Lucretia*, the *Battle of the Marne*, distilled in an intimate and profound co-operation between poet and actors, crystallized directly into dramatic substance. Great as was their success, it was only with an elite; there was still no general public.

Other side-line theatres soon attracted attention, following the lead of the Petite Scène, such as the Rideau de Paris, the Rideau Gris (Marseille), the company recruited by Jean-Louis Barrault for Cervantes' *Numance*,[59] and finally the Théâtre des Quatre-Saisons,[60] which visited New York, under André Barsacq, former collaborator with Dullin and with the Compagnie des Quinze. This last group, the Théâtre des Quatre-Saisons, follows the Copeau doctrine in new and interesting arrangements—choral, plastic, choreographic, decorative in design, with freedom and precision in acting that is very faithful to Copeau. Yes, he is the creator of the poetic theatre of our dreams; now all we have to do is to make use of it.

Finally, two years ago when Édouard Bourdet,[61] author of brilliant bourgeois satires, took over the direction of the Comédie-Française, he gave the actual production over to Copeau, Jouvet, Dullin, and Baty. Thus did Copeau's reform enter the inmost shrine. It is still too soon to know how far it will change the rituals, but at least it has now won a public.

All the writers whose works form the repertory of these various theatres seek to restore poetic drama in the spirit of Copeau's reform. This does not include Stève Passeur's sombre realistic drama, nor Gabriel Marcel's powerfully intellectual interpretation of bourgeois realism, nor François Mauriac's first attempt at theatre, *Asmodée*[62]—which is, perhaps unfortunately, identical ethically and aesthetically with his novelistic approach.

These three writers are no doubt capable of giving new life and power to this still popular genre, but in my opinion it remains a false genre. There are, however, others who have gone back to the true dramatic tradition, our hope and our disappointment.

Among the older writers is Paul Fort, who has applied the Shakespearean chronicle form to French history with excessive use of imagery; Saint-Georges de Bouhélier, whose high aims were frustrated by serious technical defects; and François Porché, whose verse-plays had only a partial success. There is Paul Demasy,[63] author of *The Tragedy of Alexander*, and of *Milmont*; Raynal's too theatrical austerity; Jean Variot's vital *Belle of Haguenau;* and the magic of Alexandre Arnoux.[64]

Then there is Jean Cocteau, that unique virtuoso, that juggler, hypnotist, wonder-worker, who could create the marvel of his *Orpheus* . . . and yet delight in perverse horrors. Jean Sarment, a potential Musset, has never attained again the exquisite charm of his *Fisher of Shadows*;[65] Marcel Achard, too, has lost his light and dreamy irony, laced with wit—the *Corsair* is an artistic, the *Adam* a moral disappointment. But Armand Salacrou[66] has grown: there is more fullness and poetry in *The Earth is Round*, a powerful re-creation of Savonarola's Florence, than in the earlier *Inconnue d'Arras*. André Josset's[67] *Elizabeth* was magnificent, but his second play inferior. *Thieves' Carnival*,[68] however, that gay and subtle fantasy of Jean Anouilh, is a great source of hope.

I must not forget the bright Parisian poetry of René Benjamin's comedy, nor the oversubtle Jean Giraudoux.[69] It would take a whole chapter, however, to do him justice. At moments he attains to tremendous power, but

too often his plays are swamped with sparkling floods of
paradox, pun, and wit. To some he is the re-creator of
tragedy; to me Giraudoux himself, not his characters,
alone speaks on the stage, but—with what poetry!

André Obey's truly tragic art, powerful, objective, living, full of poetry, is essentially created for the stage. I
mentioned him earlier, but today what has he to hope
for, without his company of actors, the Quinze? Their
director, Michel Saint-Denis, has left them to found a
dramatic school in London, and they have broken up;
Obey has lost his instrument. Yet aside from Claudel, he
is the only poetic playwright who has persevered in the
face of prejudice and failure and who has at least twice
achieved his ambition in all its purity and grandeur.

To sum up, the poetic theatre is only beginning its
career. Sooner or later it will attain full stature.

As you know, I have tried to serve this poetic theatre
as a Christian, a Catholic, although from time to time
I have still experimented in fantasy and comedy on a
nonconfessional level.[70] The year after I gave the talks
about dramatic art at the Vieux-Colombier, I founded
the acting group of the Compagnons de Notre-Dame
(1925-1930) in Paris. Our aim was to show to the amateur
stage, the critics, and the general public Christian drama.
"For the faith, for dramatic art, for dramatic art in the
spirit of faith"—was our motto. In six years we produced
twenty-one plays. The last was given in the Sainte
Chapelle, the *Mystery of Saint Louis the King*. Then I
handed the work over to my friend Henri Brochet. He
had founded the Compagnons de Jeux, a special group
of the Compagnons de Notre Dame which produced the
periodical, *Jeux, Tréteaux et Personnages*. Brochet carried

on the work I had begun, deepening and perfecting it in the *The Way of the Cross, Christmas on the Village Square, Ruth and Boaz, Susanna and the Elders.*[71]

Then we broke out of the closed theatre-house to play before crowds in the open air, in squares and on church steps for feast days, great pilgrimages and congresses. Our first attempt was on the lake shore of Annecy, *The Marvelous History of Saint Bernard of Menthon.* Today we cannot keep track of them all. Our wildest dreams have come true at Chartres, Tancremont, Liége, Cordemoy, Chaumont, Paris, Lourdes, Reims, Pontmain, Quebec, and last of all in Saint-Laurent, Canada. Specialized movements, the Jecists and Jocists, have seconded our mission. Thanks to the development of choral recitation, our "Mysteries" meet the supreme standard of Greek tragedy on its own level of truth. Sometimes the whole multitude joins with the choral speakers, thousands of voices answering the protagonists. The murmur that Copeau had desired to hear from his audience has risen to a mighty shout. Unity has been reborn.

I cannot prophesy for tomorrow. What I did prophesy yesterday has come to pass. Writers are still too few, but new instruments are at our disposal.[72] And an audience is waiting. Christian Canada has joined forces with Christian France for the renewal of a great and truly Christian drama.

There is also the initiative taken by Léon Chancerel,[73] a direct disciple of Copeau, in the Boy Scout movement. The marvelous improvisations of his Comédiens Routiers give the young a taste for poetic acting, raising secular entertainment to the level of a religious celebration like the pageants of the Jecists, the Jocists, and our own acting groups. Finally I must honor the memory of that poet, playwright, and musician, Claude Duboscq, whose wholly unclassifiable masterpiece, *Colombe la petite*, is something wholly new, moving from poetry to song, from song to dance without ever breaking the thread of the drama. May other writers follow his inspiration!

There is a great potential of diversity in Christian dramatic art as I dream of it, diversity in form and in theme. It is not imprisoned in any one formula, but infinitely adaptable, capable of expressing our faith in tragedy, comedy, farce, mystery play, pageant—as wide in its variety of forms as dramatic art itself. And for its theme, it has all humanity—all this earth with heaven and hell besides. All that is its kingdom. Who cannot feel at home there? How can we call it in any sense a "diminution"?

NOTES

These are for the most part translator's footnotes; author's footnotes will be indicated as such. Here, as throughout the text, plays are given in their original French title where no English translation is known to exist.

1. Jacques Copeau (1879-1949) opened the Théâtre du Vieux-Colombier in 1913 in opposition to the realistic theatre. The first World War interrupted his success, but after bringing his actors to the Garrick Theatre in New York from 1917-1919, he returned to Paris and renewed the Vieux-Colombier, making the stage a model for usefulness, simplicity, flexibility, and continuing to produce important experimental work. Ghéon discusses his later career in the Appendix.

2. Marie Desmares Champmeslé (1642-1698) played the title roles of Racine's *Berenice, Athalie, Phaedra,* and the part of Monime in *Mithridates;* Marguerite Duparc (1635?-1668), one of Molière's greatest actresses, played the part of Axiane in Racine's *Alexander.* [Racine took her from Molière to act at the Hôtel de Bourgogne where in 1667 she played the title role of Andromache.]

3. Jean Sully (1841-1916), known as Mounet-Sully, played all the great tragic roles of the French classical repertory; Julia Bartet (1854-1941), a French actress, trained at the Conservatoire.

4. Arnould Gréban (fl. 1456), *Passion,* a New Testament Mystery play of 70,000 lines, *circa* 1450. Revised by Jehan Michel (d. 1493), it was produced at Angers in 1486.

5. *Author's note: Commedia dell'arte* does eliminate the

author—and in consequence it is an inferior and short-lived genre.

6. Rutebeuf (1230?-1285?), a medieval minstrel, whose chief play, *The Miracle of Théophile,* was revived at the Sorbonne in 1930 by "Les Théophiliens," the students of Gustave Cohen. Jean Michel (d. 1493), accredited with a *Resurrection,* a 20-000-line Mystery play, and with the revision of Gréban's *Passion.*

7. Charles Péguy (1873-1914), founder and editor of *Les Cahiers de la quinzaine,* poet.

8. Etienne Jodelle (1532-1573), the first neoclassicist of the French stage, inspired by Italian Renaissance dramatists such as Giraldi Cintio. The *Pléiade:* Pierre de Ronsard, Jean Daurat, Jodelle, Rémy Belleau, Joachim du Bellay, Jean Antoine de Baïf, and Pontus de Tyard—a sixteenth-century group of poets who sought to classicize French language and literature.

9. Louis des Masures (1523?-1574), *Tragédies saintes, David combattant—David triomphant—David fugitif,* crit. ed. by C. Conte (Paris, 1907).

10. Tirso de Molina (Gabriel Tellez, 1584-1648), author of secular and religious plays, including *El Burlador de Sevilla,* a Don Juan play, and *El condenado por desconfiado* (*Damned for Lack of Confidence*); Lope Felix de Vega Carpio (1562-1635), creator of the classic form of Spanish play; Pedro Calderón de la Barca (1600-1681), theological poet and dramatist, *La vida es sueño* (*Life is a Dream*), *La devoción de la Cruz* (*Devotion to the Cross*), etc.

11. *Auto Sacramental,* Spanish religious play, dealing allegorically with the Mystery of the Mass, generally performed with fine music and lavish setting on the feast of Corpus Christi.

12. Racine, *Britannicus,* Act V, Scene 6:
            "Arrêtez, Néron: j'ai deux mots à vous dire."

13. Pierre Carlet de Chamblain de Marivaux (1688-1763), French dramatist, creator of a peculiarly paradoxical and stilted style called *marivaudage.*

14. By Corneille (*Le Menteur,* 1643).

15. Molière, *The Doctor in Spite of Himself* (*Le Médicin malgré lui,* 1666), Act I, Scene I. This and other citations in the text have been translated for this book.

16. Corneille, *Cinna,* Act I, Scene I:
    "Impatient désir d'une illustre vengeance,"
    Racine, *Andromache,* Act I, Scene I:
    "Qui, puisque je retrouve un ami si fidèle,"
    Racine, *Athalie,* Act I, Scene I:
    "Oui, je viens dans son temple adorer l'Éternel"
17. Molière, *The Doctor in Spite of Himself,* Act I, Scene I.
18. Plays given at the Fairs of Saint-Germain in the spring and of St. Laurent in the fall, in temporary theatres called the *Forains,* developed into permanent playhouses in Paris during the seventeenth and eighteenth centuries. The Comédie-Italienne combined with these *Forains* to form the Opéra-Comique. After the Revolution several small but important playhouses were established on the Boulevard du Temple, which revived the *Forains* and the old *Parades,* scenes given on balconies to entice the public to the play. At the height of their success they were destroyed in 1862 by Haussmann's plans for rebuilding Paris.
19. Eugène Labiche (1815-1888), *The Italian Straw Hat,* English version by L. and T. Hoffman (*The Modern Theatre,* vol. 3, ed. Eric Bentley, 1957), *Perrichon's Journey,* etc. Georges Courteline (1861-1929) and Georges Feydeau (1862-1921), writers of comedy and farce.
20. Denis Diderot (1713-1784), editor of the *Encyclopédie,* critic, exponent of bourgeois drama; Pierre Claude Nivelle de La Chaussée (1692-1754), successful writer of sentimental plays; Michel Jean Sedaine (1719-1797), a protégé of the painter David and the architect Buron, author of light-opera librettos and of bourgeois drama.
21. Jean François Ducis (1733-1816), dramatist, first adaptor of Shakespeare for the French stage.
22. Henri Bataille (1872-1922), devotee of triangle plays, "boulevard theatre," with appeal to the prurient: *Dame Nature* (1908), *The Torches* (1912).
23. Triboulet, character in Victor Hugo's five-act play, *Le Roi s'amuse;* Marion Delorme, title role in Hugo's play of the same name.
24. Frédéric Lemaître (1800-1876), the nineteenth-century popular actor, created parts such as Don César in *Don César de*

Bazan by Dumanoir and D'Ennery (1844), and Toussaint in Lamartine's *Toussaint-L'Ouverture* (1850). Sarah Bernhardt, pseudonym for Rosine Bernhard (1844-1923), achieved her fame largely in the plays of Victorien Sardou (1831-1908).

25. Auguste Maquet (1813-1888), author of *Les Vertes-Feuilles* (1862), *Dettes de coeur* (1880).

26. Eugène Scribe (1791-1861), mass-producer of intrigue comedies.

27. Guillaume Victor Émile Augier (1820-1889), with François Ponsard (1814-1887), among the first French dramatists to revolt against the excesses of the Romantics.

28. Henri François Becque (1837-1899), a naturalist in Zola's "slice of life" tradition; his best plays are *The Vultures* (*Les Corbeaux,* 1882) and *Woman of Paris* (*La Parisienne,* 1885).

29. "It is probable that, about 1610, performances were given only twice a week, except on special occasions. In Molière's time, his troupe, and probably those of his rivals, acted regularly three times a week." Henry Carrington Lancaster, *A History of French Dramatic Literature in the Seventeenth Century,* Part I, Vol. II (Baltimore: 1929), p. 713.

30. André Antoine (1858-1943), actor, producer, manager, leader in reform, founder of the Théâtre Libre (1887-1894) for production of naturalistic drama. In 1890 he produced Ibsen's *Ghosts,* followed by plays by Hauptmann, Strindberg, Björnson, etc. His revolution in acting and set design greatly influenced theatre in Europe and America.

31. Georges de Porto-Riche (1849-1930), a poetic dramatist, *Amoureuse* (1891). Henry Bernstein (1876-1953), *The Thief* (*Le Voleur,* 1907).

32. Henri Becque.

33. François de Curel (1854-1928), a spiritual and romantic writer, *Le Repas du Lion* (1897, rewritten in 1920), *La Nouvelle Idole* (1899), and *The Savage Girl* (*La Fille Sauvage,* 1902), a symbolic drama of the spiritual history of mankind.

34. Firmin Gémier, *see* below, note 47.

35. Émile Verhaeren (1855-1916), Belgian dramatist, *Les Aubes* (*Dawn,* 1898), an impressionistic play about peace.

36. Francis Vielé-Griffin (1864-1937).

37. André Gide's (1869-1951) first play was *Saül* (1896), published in 1902 and presented by Copeau in 1922.

38. Maurice de Faramond, author of *Noblesse de la terre;* Paul Hervieu (1857-1915), *La Course du Flambeau* (1901), a thesis play.

39. Paul Bourget (1852-1936), *Un divorce, La Crise,* etc., thesis plays; Edmond Rostand (1868-1918).

40. Jean Marie Mathias Philippe Auguste, Comte de Villiers de l'Isle-Adam (1838-1889), *The Revolt* and *The Escape* (translated into English by T. Barclay, Chicago, 1901); Élémir Bourges (1852-1925), *Les oiseaux s'envolent et les fleurs tombent;* Joséphin Péladan (1859-1918), *Sémiramis* (Paris, 1904), *St. Francis of Assisi* (translated by H. J. Massingham, New York, 1913).

41. Aurélien-Marie Lugné-Poë (1869-1940), actor and manager, worked with Antoine at the Théâtre Libre and Paul Fort at the Théâtre d'Art, later the Théâtre de l'Oeuvre (1892-1929); the first to produce Claudel's *Tidings Brought to Mary* (1912).

42. Henri de Régnier (1864-1936), novelist and poet, author of *Scènes mythologiques* (Paris, 1924). Francis Jammes (1868-1938).

43. Alfred Jarry (1873-1907), *Ubu Roi* (1896); *Ubu Enchaîné* was produced only in 1937.

44. Henri Ghéon, *Nos directions, réalisme et poésie, notes sur le drame poétique, du classicisme, sur le vers libre* (Paris, Nouvelle revue française, 1911).

45. Paul Claudel (1868-1955), poet-dramatist. *L'Échange,* an early play, produced in London as *The Exchange,* 1915; *The Satin Slipper* (tr. G. O'Connor, Sheed and Ward, 1945), *Tidings Brought to Mary* (tr. L. M. Sill, Yale University Press, 1916), *The City* (tr. L. S. Newberry, Yale University Press, 1920), etc.

46. Robert de Flers (1872-1927) and Gaston Armand de Caillavet (1869-1915), collaborators in light satirical comedy, like Henri Meilhac (1831-1897) and Ludovic Halévy (1834-1908) in Offenbach librettos. Alfred Capus (1858-1922), *Rosine, La Veine* (1901), *L'Attentat;* Maurice Donnay (1859-1945), *Amants.*

47. Firmin Gémier (1866-1934), director at the Comédie des Champs-Elysées and later the Odéon; Edward Gordon Craig

(1872-   ), original producer and designer of great influence in Germany and America especially. Craig was a follower of Adolphe Appia (1862-1928), scenic interpreter of Wagner, author of *La mise en scène du drame Wagnérien* (1895), whose work is the antithesis of naturalism.

48. Max Reinhardt (1873-1943), German director and producer of massive and extravagant productions; Jacques Rouché, director of the Opéra (1914), of the Opéra-Comique (1937), and later of the Théâtre des Arts. Serge Diaghilev (1872-1929); Constantin Stanislavski (C. S. Alexeyev, 1863-1938).

49. Réné Benjamin (1885-1948), *Les Plaisirs du Hasard* (1922); Jules Romains (1885-   ), *Knock (Dr. Knock,* 1924), a satire, and *Donogoo* (1930); Marcel Achard (1899-   ), *Jean de la lune, Corsaire* (1938).

50. The Théâtre de l'Atelier, an experimental theatre opened by Charles Dullin (1885-1949); the Comédie des Champs-Elysées, founded by Jacques Hebertot in 1913; in 1923 his Studio specialized in experimental productions; Gaston Baty (1885-1952) worked with Firmin Gémier at the Comédie des Champs-Elysées and at the Odeón, a national theatre, directed also at the Studio and later at the Théâtre Montparnasse and La Chimère.

51. This refers to Ghéon's return to the practice of religion during World War I.

52. Jean Thorel (Raymond Bouthors) (1859-1916), translator and playwright; his play *Devant le bonheur* (1898) received an award from the French Academy.

53. *Author's note: La Bergère au pays des Loups* [*St. Germaine of the Wolf Country,* translated by F. L. Sheed (London, 1932)] at the Cercle in Luxembourg.

54. Henri Brochet (1898-   ), actor and dramatist (*St. Anne and the Gouty Rector and other Plays,* tr. M. S. Goldman and O. R. Goldman, New York, 1950).

55. *The Marvelous History of St. Bernard,* translated by B. V. Jackson (London and New York: 1933).

56. Sacha Guitry (1885-1957), author of light comedies.

57. Baty and Dullin, see above, note 50. Louis Jouvet (1887-1952), actor and producer, with Copeau in New York, 1917-1919; later in the Comédie des Champs-Elysées, L'Athénée (1934), the

Conservatoire (1935), and producer of the Comédie-Française (1936). Georges Pitoëff (1887-1939), a Russian actor, with his wife Ludmilla founded a company at the Théâtre des Arts, later at the Mathurins.

58. André Obey (1892-   ), dramatist whose early plays were written for Copeau and the Compagnie des Quinze under the directorship of Michel Saint-Denis, Copeau's nephew; John Gielgud played *Noah* in the 1935 London production.

59. Jean-Louis Barrault (1910-   ), French actor and producer, pupil of Dullin at l'Atelier, member of the Comédie-Française, 1940-1946, then founder of his own acting company.

60. The Théâtre des Quatre-Saisons grew out of the Compagnie des Quinze under the leadership of André Bakst and André Barsacq.

61. Édouard Bourdet (1877-1944).

62. *Asmodée* (1939) was produced in New York in 1958, and the *Egoists* (*Les Malaimés,* 1945) in 1959.

63. Paul Fort (1872-   ) organized the Théâtre d'Art in 1891; Saint-Georges de Bouhélier (1876-   ), *Le Carnaval des Enfants; François Porché* (1877-1945), *La Dauphine* (produced by Copeau, 1921). Paul Demasy (1884-   ), *La Tragédie d'Alexandre* (1912-1919) and *Milmort* (1933).

64. Paul Raynal (1882-1951), *Le maître de son coeur* (1920), *The Unknown Warrior* (1924). Jean James Variot (1881-   ), *La Belle de Haguenau, comédie légendaire* (Paris, 1922), *Boumpernickel* (Paris, 1933), *La Téméraire* (Paris, 1938); Alexandre Arnoux (1884-   ), *Hugh of Bordeaux* (*Huon de Bordeaux,* 1922) and *Petite Lumière et l'Ours* (1924), produced by Dullin.

65. Jean Cocteau (1889-   ); Jean Sarment, *La Couronne de Carton* (produced in 1920 by Lugné-Poë), *Pêcheur d'Ombres* (1921).

66. Armand Salacrou (1900-   ), *The Earth Is Round* (*La terre est ronde,* 1937).

67. André Josset, author of *Elizabeth, la femme sans homme* (Paris, 1936), *Les Borgia, famille étrange* (Paris, 1938).

68. Jean Anouilh (1910-   ), *Thieves' Carnival* (*Bal des Voleurs,* 1932).

69. Jean Giraudoux (1882-1944).

70. *Author's note:* For lack of space I do not mention my experiments in religious plays for nonbelievers [*le peuple infidèle*], such as *Le Comédien* [*The Comedian,* tr. A. Bland (London: 1933)], *Judith,* etc.

71. *Author's note:* I will not list here all the other groups that have followed our example, except the ambitious Compagnons de Saint Laurent in Canada.

72. *Author's note:* To tell the truth, some of us are attempting to Christianize the bourgeois-realist theatre, and with success. But that is another story.

73. Léon Chancerel (1886-   ), dramatist and producer, pupil of Copeau, founded (1929) the Comédiens Routiers. In 1935 he renamed the Vieux-Colombier as Le Théâtre de l'Oncle Sebastien for production of plays for children, written or adapted by himself. Today the theatre is again known as the Vieux-Colombier.

DRAMABOOKS

CRITICISM